FOOTPRINTS
IN THE
SAND

A Memoir

Do they have any meaning or importance?
Will anyone even remember?
Everyone talks to God. The key is knowing how to listen.

Robert R. Grant

USMC Vietnam, 1968, Tet offensive survivor

ISBN 978-1-63885-849-2 (Hardcover)
ISBN 978-1-63885-848-5 (Digital)

Covenant Books
11661 Hwy 707
Murrells Inlet, SC 29576
www.covenantbooks.com

CHAPTER 1

Vietnam 1967–1968

This is a story about a small boy who had a bad experience at two different churches. I felt I couldn't trust preachers, pastors, or priests. Because of those bad experiences, I decided not to go to church ever again. My relationship with the good Lord was a bit shaky. It wasn't until I got to Vietnam that I was reunited with God. I made a promise to God. This book will tell the story of how that promise changed my life.

Vietnam, a place far, far away, was nothing like any place I had ever seen or could even imagine. I grew up in a four-bedroom, three-bath home near Lake Harriet in South Minneapolis. I thought everyone went to bed with clean sheets and had three square meals a day. Vietnam was quite an eye-opener.

On the plane going over, I knew I was trained by one of the best: the United States Marine Corps. I had thrown grenades and qualified on the rifle range. I put ten out of ten in the bull's-eye at five hundred meters, which qualified me as an expert. Training was tough, but when you are through, you are in the best physical shape you could possibly be in. They did their very best to get you ready for the very worst, physically and mentally.

When I left the States and headed toward Vietnam, I had a lot of time to think about what was ahead of me. I had never gone deer hunting; in fact, I never fired a gun until I got into the Marine

Corps. I wondered how I would react my first time in combat. I knew I could take any weapon apart, clear it, and put it back together blindfolded. I was well trained but had no idea what I was getting myself into. I was venturing into new territory.

I had heard all the stories from the guys returning from Vietnam. I asked myself if it could really be that bad. Little did I know, it was going to be much worse.

After landing in Okinawa, we received our final shots, which included an array of immunizations and anticoagulants to thicken our blood so that if we were injured, we wouldn't bleed out. Then we were on our way to Vietnam. We flew a commercial airliner into Da Nang. The plane was made up of 120 Marines from many different units.

From Da Nang, I took a C1-17 to Chu Lai, a Marine air base just south of Da Nang near the South China Sea. I was assigned to the VMA-121, the Green Knights, which was originally commissioned as a fighter squadron on June 24, 1941, four days after the Japanese attack on Pearl Harbor. The Green Knights had an impressive record as a top Marine squadron. Captain Foss, the second leading ace in Marine Corps history, scored twenty-six enemy kills and was awarded the Congressional Medal of Honor. VMA was awarded both the Presidential Unit Citation and the Navy Unit Citation.

Returning to Chu Lai in September 1967, the Green Knights continued their impressive record as top Marine attack squadron. Lieutenant Colonel William D. Shippen was commanding officer. Born on January 29, 1929, he was from Arkansas and had a wife and three sons. The executive officer was Lt. Colonel G. H. Barlow from Alabama.

When I arrived at VMA-121, I was not greeted with open arms. In fact, no one wanted to talk to me. They didn't want to know your name, if you were married, or if you had a family. This was my experience for almost a month until I asked what was going on. The sergeant told me it was much easier to zip up that body bag when you didn't know the person inside. I found that to be true. I only wish they had told me that when I first arrived.

My first day in Vietnam is one I will never forget. I also didn't know there would be many more to come. A Marine corporal took a picture of me. He said, "I thought I'd get a picture, not knowing how long you're going to be here." I look back at that picture…my clothes were clean, I didn't look all grubby, and I didn't smell.

Shortly after that picture was taken, I reported to the sergeant. As he started to show me around, the Vietcong dropped in a barrage of mortars. The sergeant and three men took off running. Not knowing where to go, I followed them. Just then, I was picked up, thrown backward through the air, and landed on my back. I couldn't breathe because the wind was knocked out of me. My eyes were burning, and I hurt from head to toe. It felt as if I had been hit by a bus.

As I wiped my eyes and started to see, I saw blood all over my hands. The first thing I thought was, *It's my first day in this country, and I'm going to die.* I could hear screaming around me. I was not prepared for any of this and began to panic. As I started to catch my breath, someone grabbed me and said, "Get over here and help!"

A Marine to my left had bad injuries, and I was told to put pressure on the wound. After the Marine was airlifted out by chopper, I realized the blood that covered me from head to toe was not mine. It was the blood of the Marine right in front of me who was badly injured.

Later that day, we were sitting around, and one of the Marines opened a can of beans. My mind started to process what I experienced that day. It was so overwhelming that my body couldn't handle it. I found myself puking my guts out over in the weeds. The sergeant came over and said, "Don't worry, Private, you will get over that." The sad thing was, he was right.

Bob Grant, Viet Nam, 1968

The young boy that arrived in that new country that day would never exist again. The sergeant told me, "You have thirty days to come online. Get your mind in tune with everything around you. At that point, you will no longer think about what to do. You will react without hesitation. If you make it to that point, your chances of survival will go way up."

The food had a lot to be desired, and the water was even worse. It tasted like warm pool water with extra chlorine added. I didn't eat much and probably drank less. We were supposed to take malaria pills every day, but the pills caused diarrhea, so not many Marines took them. I found myself becoming weaker and weaker by the day. Because of the incoming or outgoing shelling every day, no one ever got more than an hour or two of sleep at night. We operated twelve hours on and twelve hours off.

Once at the end of the twelve-hour shift, I found myself running a high fever. The monsoons had already started. It rained for about thirty days straight, and everything was wet. I found myself in a tent, lying on a pallet and trying to stay off the wet ground. I started to shiver. For twelve hours I lay there without moving, except I couldn't stop shivering. Then I started to shake. My body was doing everything it could to create heat. At the end of twenty-four hours, the shaking stopped, and I thought I was finally getting better. Little did I know that my body had dropped to such a low temperature that I was in trouble. I was so weak I couldn't move. At some point, I became unconscious.

One of the Marines must have stopped to check on me and found me unresponsive. I woke up in a surgical hospital, the 91st Evac Hospital north of Chu Lai. I was not sure how I got there or what exactly was wrong with me. When the doctor came by, he told me I had a blood infection, and my white count was very low. I was so weak lying on the cot that I could not move. For a short period of time, I thought I was safe. Little did I know that the Vietcong would drop mortars on the surgical unit every day. As the mortar started falling, all the doctors, nurses, and anyone that could move ran out to the bunkers. After the doctor came back into the tent, he said he had a shot for me.

He said, "It's really going to hurt. Do you want it in the arm or the rump?"

"The arm is fine," I said.

When I got the shot, I said, "That didn't hurt."

He smiled and said, "Give it a minute."

All of a sudden, it was like someone hit my arm with a baseball bat.

The doctor said, "That pain will move through your whole body, from your head to your toes. When it reaches your heart, it will slow your heart rate way down. If it gets too slow, I will have to put this needle in your heart and inject adrenaline to get it going."

The pain was unbelievable! When it reached my lungs, I could hardly breathe. Thank God he never stuck that needle in my chest. I don't know how long it took, but it seemed like hours. I have often wondered what he injected me with and what it did to me.

Some of the wounded in the MASH unit did not move or make a sound. The critical were transported out to a hospital ship off the coast. There were two hospital ships. When one got full, it would leave and go to Japan. After unloading all the patients, it would return to Vietnam. The problem was, the fighting in 1967 and 1968 was the worst in the history of the war. The second hospital ship filled up and headed to Japan while the first hospital ship was still on its way back. There was no place to send the critically wounded. The Marine next to me had about ten tubes coming out of him, and the top of his head had been removed and sewn back on. He did not move or make a sound. He should've been on one of those hospital ships in intensive care.

While I recovered at the MASH unit, they put me to work to help get my strength back. I would help carry the wounded off the choppers into the tent. There were two wooden sawhorses that we would place the cots on. There the surgeons would do their best to stabilize the soldiers. Surgical rooms made up of tents and sawhorses were unbelievable; these conditions were unacceptable, but they were the best we had.

Just before I headed back to my unit, a doctor came and said, "Jump in the Jeep. I think you'll like this." What I didn't know was that Bob Hope and his Christmas show were at American Division close by.

Bob Hope and Raquel Welch, 1967, Viet Nam

They had an area roped off for the wounded that was close to the stage. There was Bob Hope and Raquel Welch standing so close that I could see the color of her eyes. All I could think about was making it back home and finding a beautiful, round-eyed girl that looked like that. Little did I know that many moons later, God would answer my prayers, and I would meet my soulmate. Every year after, I would watch the *Bob Hope Christmas Show*. Bob Hope would venture into hostile territory in the middle of Vietnam to give all the service men and women overseas a touch of Christmas. My heart went out to each and every one of them. I know what they were feeling because I had been there and done that.

When I got back to my unit in Chu Lai, the word was out that something big was going down. We knew there were many Vietcong in the area. Many years later, an admiral in the Navy gave me a set of books by *Life* magazine detailing the history of Vietnam. In those books, it stated eighty thousand Vietcong hit all major bases up and down the coast.

We thought the attack would come on our New Year's Day, January 1. Nothing big went down. The Vietcong only did major attacks at night. They hit-and-run during the day. It was Tuesday, January 30, 1968. All was quiet until 4:00 a.m. What we didn't know was that the Vietcong had stripped, shaved their bodies, covered themselves with sap, and rolled in the sand. Carrying a satchel of explosives, they crawled right between our bunkers. We never saw them. At 4:00 a.m. sharp, they dropped a satchel full of explosives down one of the air vents to our bomb dump. We had enough ordinance and bombs to supply three squadrons of aircraft. This included a squadron of A-4 Skyhawks, a squadron of F-4 Phantoms, and a squadron of A-6 Intruders. An A-6 intruder would hold twenty-eight 250-pound bombs every time it went up. I can only imagine how much ordinance was in that bunker when it exploded. It was like 12 o'clock in the morning—so bright you thought you were looking up at the sun. Less than a second later, the ground started to shake like a freight train was going over my bunker. At that very moment, I thought for sure I was going to die.

Southern most hanger damaged from bomb dump explosion

"God?" I asked. "If you get me out of this mess, I will spend the rest of my life being the best person I can be."

I had been in Vietnam about three months when the Tet Offensive occurred. I still had ten months to go to find out if the good Lord would grant my request.

Rick W. Hall, a fellow Marine out of La Mesa, California, was in the bunker with me. He dropped his weapon and said, "We're dead."

I got upset with him and replied, "Maybe so, but pick up that weapon. We're going to take as many of them with us as we can."

After the initial explosion, here comes Charlie, which is what we called the Vietcong. One thing that might have saved us was an underground fuel cell that held the aviation fuel for all three squadrons. This was located just to the right of our bunker. Just a few seconds after the explosion, the fuel cell exploded; two hundred feet of burning aviation fuel skyrocketed into the air. We were just north of the fuel cell, and the wind was blowing south. The heat was so intense we could feel it inside of our bunker. When Charlie started to attack, the heat was so intense that they stayed clear of the fuel cell and our bunker.

The Tet Offensive lasted about seven days. At the end of the Tet, an information bulletin, No. 33 RVN, was sent out:

> Marine Attack Squadron 121
> Marine Attack Group 12
> 1st Marine Aircraft Wing, F.M.F. Pac
> FPO, San Francisco 96602
> Commanding Officer Lt. Col. R. J. Kern
> Executive Officer Lt. Col. J. W. Miller

> General Westmoreland's Congratulatory Message

A. I extend my personal congratulations and covey as well the official commendations of the Military Assistance Command, Vietnam, to the men and woman of the command for outstanding professional performance during the period of the enemy's TET Aggression beginning 29 January 1968.

B. Your alertness, aggressiveness, professionalism, and courage—individually, by team, and by unit—adds new luster to your outstanding reputation. During the week, in conjunction with the forces of the Republic of Vietnam and our free World Allies, you have blunted the enemy's offensive and turned the tables on him. YOU HAVE DESTROYED MORE OF THE ENEMY IN SEVEN DAYS THAN THE UNITED STATES HAS LOST IN THE LAST SEVEN YEARS OF THE WAR SINCE I JANUARY 1961.

C. I know you share my respect for the admirable performance of our Vietnam and Free World Comrades in Arms in our mutual triumph. We are proud to fight side by side with such Allies.

D. But we cannot relax for a moment. We must continue to stand ready for the enemy's second wave of attack. As you maintain your resolute alert for what may come next and go on the offensive, again let me assure you of my profound pride in you conduct and performance and my confidence that the defeats we are inflicting on the enemy may measurably shorten the war.

I still have that letter from General Westmoreland, and that one sentence says it all.

As the time went on, I was convinced I was going to die in this hellhole called Vietnam. My brother wrote me from back home and said he was going to get married. He wanted to know when I would be arriving home from my thirteen-month tour. I don't remember my exact words, but whatever I said convinced him I was going to die there. The only way I would be coming home was in a body bag. He went ahead and got married.

At the time, I didn't give a lot of thought. Months later, when I received the wedding pictures and saw everyone having a great time back home, it hit me. I knew I must let it go to keep my edge.

As time went on in Vietnam, I became very hard-core. The fear was gone. Everyone knew this day was coming. We were just existing from day to day. Sometimes seconds seemed like hours, and minutes seemed like days; it was like you had no purpose. You just existed from day to day. There wasn't really anything to look forward to. I got one three-minute phone call by shortwave radio in the 395 days I was there. I called my mom. My father was dead, and my brother was now married. I wondered how my mom was dealing with all this. I enjoyed talking to my mom, but when the phone call was over, I sat there thinking about life. I wondered what God had in store for me. He got me through the Tet Offensive, so God must have had plans for me. I wondered if I would ever make it home.

It wasn't until I had finished my twelfth month that the fear came back. I started to think I might make it home alive. I was down to my last day in the country after 395 days total. I had to take a C1-17 out of Chu Lai to Da Nang. I think there were eight of us flying out that day on that C1-17. As the wheels came up, and we were out over hostile territory, we started to take rounds of small arms fire. Just a few minutes into the flight, the right engine started to smoke and caught on fire. They had to shut it down, so we were flying on just one engine. I wondered if we would make it to Da Nang.

They opened the side door, and the red light above the door came on. We all stood up and hooked up to that strap that automatically opens your shoot when you bail out. The NCO told us that if the green light came on, we were all going out that door. I said to myself, "This can't be happening." I knew if I went out that door that I would never make it home. I looked up and said to God, "I hope you're still with me." We made it to Da Nang on one engine. I knew I was one step closer, but I was not out of Vietnam yet.

To get out of Da Nang to Okinawa, we flew commercial airliners. The continental aircraft, a 727 jet, took fire coming into Da Nang. The pilot got the bird on the deck, but it was too damaged to fly out. There we sat. We had 120 Marines ready to fly home, but our aircraft was in a down status. We thought we would just wait till the next one arrived the next day. Not so—there were another 120 men assigned to that aircraft. This went on for five days. The lieutenant colonel in charge of us said, "Saddle up. We are going out on the tarmac."

He went inside to the control tower and told whoever was in charge that when the new plane landed, and they opened the doors for the 120 men to get off, he was going to turn his Marines loose on the 120 sailors waiting to get on that aircraft. The 120 that were still standing could get on the plane. Of course, it would be a nightmare trying to figure out who was on the plane and who was not. They would have to assign that plane to us, or they would have a real problem on their hands. When he came out, he had the paperwork, and we got on the plane.

CHAPTER 2

Leaving Okinawa and Going Home to the USA

December 1968

We landed in Okinawa, got debriefed, and got all our shots. We then caught another continental airliner, a 727 jet, and headed toward the States. It was eighteen hours of nonstop flying time from Okinawa to Travis Air Force Base in California.

When I got on the plane, the sergeant told me to sit down, look, and not touch. He was referring to the beautiful stewardesses. I fell in love with each and every one of them. They were the best. They turned first class into a sleeping area and made us all feel like we were special. Little did I know that would all change. After Travis Air Force Base, I caught a nonstop flight to Minneapolis. When I got off the plane with another fellow Marine, we were confronted by a mob of long-haired hippies. They had a mob mentality, with signs and vulgarity all directed at the military—at us. One of the long-haired freaks spat on the Marine next to me. I could see the rage in his face, and I knew this long-haired freak was about to die. Without hesitation, I slid my hand under his belt in the back and jerked it as hard as I could. He turned; now his rage was directed at me.

All I said was, "You go home. You go to jail." I repeated myself, "You go home. You go to jail."

He started to calm down. I told him that long-haired freak wasn't worth it and we needed to get out of there. We headed out of the terminal. I don't think that long-haired freak realized how close he came to dying that day. One blow to his throat would have crushed his larynx. He would not be able to make a sound or breathe, and he would have been dead in minutes.

While I was in Vietnam, my mom never told me what was happening back home. She always talked about good things that would make me happy. Little did I know that when I was in the MASH unit for those twenty to thirty days that I don't remember, my mom was sent an MIA (missing in action) letter. I never knew she got that letter. She never said a word. When she passed away at almost ninety, my wife and I were going through her things and found the letter. I can't imagine how hard that must have been. When I think back at that time, I wonder what her life was like: home alone, her husband dead, her oldest son married and moved to Michigan, and me in a MASH unit in Vietnam, unable to write home, not knowing my CO, and not knowing where I was. I can't imagine the pain she must've felt. I don't know how she received that letter. I wonder if a Marine officer and a chaplain showed up at the door. How devastating that must have been.

CHAPTER 3

Before the War

August 1966

I joined the Marine Corps on August 8, 1966. After basic training, I was sent to Camp La June, North Carolina. I was going to school to be a mechanic.

My father had gotten sick earlier that year in March. He was one of the first to have an open-heart surgery in Minnesota. Dr. David Olson, chief of staff at Eitel Hospital, was overseeing his care. He ended up having two open-heart surgeries, two leg amputations, and a procedure that consisted of severing spinal nerves so that muscles would relax and relieve the pressure around his waist so the blood could go to the legs. In November 1966, my mom wrote me a letter telling me I must come home because Dad wouldn't make it to Christmas. Along with her letter was a letter from Dr. Olson, the chief of staff at Eitel Hospital, stating Dad's condition and how long he had been in the hospital. He had spent over 120 days in intensive care. The letter listed everything my father had been through. It was a very long letter.

I took the letters to my commanding officer. He told me he would have the United Way and the Red Cross look into it. They would determine if I should receive emergency leave. The next day, I got word to report to my CO. He called me in, sat me down, and told me they had determined that Dr. Olson was a friend of the family and would say anything to get me home for Christmas. Leave denied.

A few days later, I got a call from my brother: Dad had died. I walked into the CO's office. I was already in trouble; I didn't have an appointment, and I didn't ask to see him. He stood up, and you could tell he was very upset with me.

I said, "Sir, my father's dead. Do you think his condition is serious enough now?"

I didn't wait for a response. I turned, walked out, went back to my locker, got my stuff, and walked off base. I was now absent without leave and in even more trouble. As I was walking to the airport, a black limo pulled up alongside. The window went down, and it was the chaplain. He said, "Where are you going?"

"To the airport."

"Do you have any money?"

"No."

He said, "Get in the car. I have emergency leave papers and emergency leave money."

He took me to the airport. On the way, he asked me how I was going to get a ticket if I didn't have any money. I told him that I didn't know and was going to figure that out when I got there.

When I got to Minneapolis, I told my mom I wasn't going back.

She answered, "You won't disgrace your father's name, and you are going back."

Before I had left home to go to Camp La June, North Carolina, I hadn't known if I was going to make it home for Christmas. I had bought a few things and put them in the closet so Mom could put them under the tree at Christmas. The funeral was really hard. I didn't take it well on Christmas morning when Mom asked me to hand out the presents. When I picked up the one that said "From Bob to Dad," I lost it. I did not enjoy one day or even one minute of those thirty days at home. The Marine Corps had refused to let me go home and say goodbye to my father. When he died, I asked God why I was being punished. I did not know he had a plan for me.

When I got back to Camp La June, I went back to school. I hadn't been there very long when we had a major snowstorm. The steel buildings we were housed in had no heat. All the pipes froze in the bathroom, so there was no running water and no toilets. One of the Marines that was in my building had a father who was a congressman or senator. The big black limo with the police escort and American flags on both sides of the hood pulled up to our building. His son went out to the car, got in the back, and talked for some time.

,. I found out that the base was being shut down. I was going to Memphis, Tennessee, for aviation training. I was going to be a structural mechanic and spent twelve weeks in school. When I finished school, I received papers telling me I was going to Vietnam.

CHAPTER 4

Keeping a Promise I Made to My Father on His Deathbed

My father, Sanford C. Grant

1969

When I came back from Vietnam, I reported to Beaufort, South Carolina. I learned that if I had less than 120 days left in the United States Marine Corps, they were going to send me home. This was 1969; the war was still going on. The Marine Corps didn't want the

Marines coming back to tell the Marines going over what it was like. The Marine Corps released me from active duty on April 10, 1969.

While I was in basic training and during my entire time in Vietnam, Mom kept many things from me that I did not find out until I got home. I had a hard time dealing with Dad's death, but what I did not know was that he acquired $1.3 million in medical bills. We lost the house and everything in it. We also lost my father's business, the place in Cape Coral, Florida, the boat, the two cars, the Cadillac, and the Chevrolet; everything was gone when I arrived home. Mom had thirty days to find a place to live, and she still owed $37,000 for medical bills. In 1969, that was a lot of money. They can't do that today. Now they can take everything you own except your home. When I got home, I found out we didn't have a pot to pee in.

Sanford and Leah Grant, Father and Mother

Back row, tallest 6'5"
Sanford C. Grant
Year 1954 President of the A.M.R. American
Manufacturers Representatives
My mom, front row, third from the right

My father, Sanford Colby Grant, had started his own business called Grant Brokerage Corporation. He was the president of the American Manufacturers Representatives (AMR) in 1954. His big accounts were Hi-C, Snow Crop Foods, and Spice Island. He was a good man, and I still miss him today. I can only hope God takes me quickly. To spend all that time in intensive care, to go through all that pain, to acquire all that debt, and to lose everything you spent your whole life building had to be terribly painful for my father.

A father plays a major role in a person's life. He had these little sayings that played a major role in my life: "The greatest gift is the gift of giving," "Never take more than you give," and "Always take one day at a time."

I was in sixth grade attending Clara Barton Elementary School on Forty-Third and Bryant Avenue South in South Minneapolis. Because of all the racial unrest down south, some politician thought it was a good idea to take a bunch of White students and place them in an all-Black school. I lived on Fortieth Street when they moved the new boundary to Forty-First. All my friends attended Ramsey Middle School, which was located right next to Washburn High School. I was sent to Bryant Junior High, located on E. Thirty-Eighth Street and Third Avenue South.

I was not aware of any racial tension in Minnesota. When I got to Bryant Junior High, I felt like I was the only White kid in the school. I was never treated poorly or threatened in any way. I remember my father saying to take one day at a time. Bryant Junior High had a swimming pool on the first floor. The boys would all shower in one big shower room and drink out of the same water fountain. At the end of the day, depending on the weather, I would either walk home or take the bus. It was sixteen blocks from the school to my house. If I took the bus, we would all get on the bus and sit together. It was not like down south where they separated Whites and Blacks.

At the end of my ninth grade, everyone from Bryant Junior High went to Central High School. Because of where I lived, I returned to Washburn High School. I had lost touch with all my friends from Clara Barton School. It was like starting all over. There was my father again, telling me to take one step at a time and one day at a time.

One of his other sayings was, "The greatest gift is the gift of giving." This came back to me much later in life. I had retired and moved to a small town in southern Minnesota. My wife and I moved in with our oldest daughter. One of the first days at the farm, a neighbor, John Day, came over and introduced himself. He said if we ever needed anything to give him a call. Over the next ten years, he was there to help many times. Whenever he needed a helping hand, he would call me, and I was happy to help. I bought an E-Z-Go golf cart at a garage sale for $400. John told me that if I ever wanted to sell that E-Z-Go, he would like to buy it. I was thinking of buying a used John Deere Gator for around the farm, so I called John. He came over and made me an offer on the E-Z-Go. I told him I would think about it for a day.

The next day, John showed up. I told him I wasn't going to sell him my E-Z-Go. He had a blank look on his face and didn't say anything. I could tell his bad knees were giving him a hard time. He was having trouble just getting around. I informed him I was giving him the E-Z-Go. He said no. Then he realized that was the only way he was going to get it. I drove the golf cart to his house, and he gave me a ride back to the farm. I told him the other day that every time I drove past his house and saw him and Pat out riding around on the E-Z-Go, it really made me feel good inside. It was the gift that keeps on giving. I told him that I should thank him for taking the golf cart.

My father's last saying, "Always give more than you take," comes into play in many aspects of life such as with family, friends, and even the big garden at the farm. The more we put into it, the harder we work at it, and the more we get out of it.

When I came home from basic training in September of 1966, my father was still very ill, but I was convinced everything was going to be fine. Little did I know how things were going to turn out. He made me promise to take care of Mom if anything happened to him. I told him that everything would be fine. He knew better.

The summer of 1966, before I went into the Marine Corps, I was working at May Brothers Wholesale Grocery. I didn't think I was ever going back there to work, but for some reason, I got a union withdrawal card. When I came home from the Marine Corps, I had five years seniority and was making top dollar. This was a key to helping me qualify for a home loan. With the VA-guaranteed loan, five years of experience on the job, and making enough money to qualify, I got a home loan and bought a double bungalow on 5400 James Avenue South in Minneapolis. I moved into one side of the double bungalow with my mom. I ended up working two jobs: forty-eight hours a week at May Brothers and twenty-four hours a week at Lund's Food Holdings. I only needed about four hours' sleep a night. I was lucky if I ever got that in Vietnam.

One day, Mr. Russell T. Lund called me up to his office. He said he had heard many good things about me and wanted me to come work for him full time. I told him my story. He was more interested in talking about my time in Vietnam, so we spent the next two hours talking about it. He made me feel like I was talking to my father. I learned that he treated all his employees like family. I informed him that I really needed both jobs to make things work. Mr. Lund said, "What if I match the pay of both jobs?" I accepted and spent thirty-four years working for him.

After ten years working for Mr. Lund, I had an accident at work that put me in the hospital. I couldn't walk. Mr. Lund heard lawyers had come to see me, and they told me I could collect $1 million dollars and never work another day the rest of my life. Mr. Lund came to the hospital and told me that if I needed anything to come and see him; he would take care of me. He also said my two daughters would go to Gustavus Adolphus College at no cost to me. I chose not to hire those lawyers or pursue a lawsuit; instead, I spent months in physical therapy and went back to work less than a year after my accident. When Mr. Lund Sr. died, the new CEO, Russel T. Lund III, said he had no obligation to fulfill his grandfather's wishes. I never got a dime. Pat Lund, RT, Lund Sr.'s wife, remembered her husband saying he was going to send my two daughters to college. She didn't assist me financially, but she wrote a letter of recommendation. Both Katie and Elizabeth ended up going to Gustavus Adolphus College. I didn't know at the time I joined the Eden Prairie Fire Department that the pension from the fire department would help pay for my two girls to go to college.

CHAPTER 5

Big Brothers of America

The next time God got involved in my life was when a good friend, Lon McKee, called and asked me to take over as football coach at Kenny Park. He had become ill and was unable to continue as coach. I told him my plate was full, and I wouldn't be able to help. My heart rate doubled, my blood pressure went up, I broke out in a sweat, and his voice in my head said, "What are you going to do? You promised to make a difference. Are you going to step up to the plate or walk away?" I knew it was the good Lord talking to me.

There was a pause. Lon said, "Are you still there?"

I said, "Okay I'll do it." I didn't know much about coaching, but I knew I had to do this.

Bob Grant, Football Coach

We practiced a couple days a week and had games on Saturday mornings. I had never coached before. I tried to teach the kids the basics, good sportsmanship, and most importantly, to enjoy the game. All I asked from each of the players was that they do their best. I would do my best to train them, and they would do their best on game day. That's all I could ask for. I couldn't ask for anything else. After the first game, I asked everyone to raise their hand if they did their best. They all raised their hands. I told them that made all of us winners. When I asked what winners did, no one answered.

I said, "We all go to the Dairy Queen, on me!"

I got a great response.

We ended up giving the owner of the Dairy Queen our schedule and told him we would be coming after every game. He thanked me and put on extra help, so there wouldn't be twenty-four kids in line keeping others from getting ice cream. He opened a special window just for us. The team got together at the end of the year and gave me a trophy for coach of the year. I still have it today. I have a lot of trophies from playing sports because I played till I was fifty, but the coach of the year trophy means the most to me.

Little did I know, God got me involved in coaching for a bigger reason. I received a call from an organization called Big Brothers Big Sisters of America. They asked if I ever heard of them; I said no. They told me they wanted me to be a mentor to a young boy that didn't have a father. I told them the same thing I told Lon McKee: My life is just too busy, and I don't have the time. Then it happened all over again. I broke out in a sweat, my heart rate doubled, my blood pressure went through the roof, and that voice popped into my head. "You gave your word…are you going to make a difference? What are you going to do?" I had no choice. I had made a promise to the good Lord that I would do my best to make a difference.

After a pause, the person on the phone asked, "Are you still there?

"Yes, I'll do it," I replied. "I'll be a big brother."

I met with Tom, his mother, and the Big Brothers organization. Tom's mom had to give the go-ahead before any of this would happen.

Tom O'Brien was the quarterback of the football team, so we already had a good working relationship. When football ended, we would get together once or twice a week. We would do things like play golf at Cedar Hills Golf Course in Eden Prairie, bike around Lake Harriet, or just hang out. Most of the time, I would leave it up to him. This was all new to me anyway; I had no idea what I was doing.

After some time, Tom started bringing a friend. The boy's name was Mike Longman, and he was the halfback on the football team. Tom lived only four houses down from me, and Mike lived just a block away. I played on a softball team and a broomball team. They would come and watch sometimes. My broomball team was called Tasty Pizza, and it was out of Columbia Heights. I organized and ran the team, which was made up of a few professional athletes. One was a linebacker for the Denver Broncos, another was a tight end for Atlanta, and Ronnie Kulas was a tight end for the Golden Gophers and made all-conference. The only weak link on the team was probably me.

We won seven out of eight tournaments one year and ended up in the world broomball tournament sponsored by Budweiser. There were over one hundred teams entering the tournament. Most of the games were played at ice arenas around the city, but the final sixteen teams played at the St. Paul Civic Center. When we made it to the civic center, most of the other teams had already been eliminated. The tournament was down to the final eight, and we had a game at 9:00 a.m. on Saturday. Ronnie Kulas, one of the members of the team, was getting married. Unfortunately, his stag party was the Friday night before our game.

Because I ran the ball club, I ordered the jerseys. Tom O'Brien, my little brother from Big Brothers Big Sisters of America, was our equipment manager for the broomball team. Even though he was about twelve at the time, I had ordered him a complete uniform.

It was just like my own, except he was only about five feet tall and weighed one hundred pounds soaking wet.

We were supposed to play Great Lakes Paper Co. out of Canada that Saturday morning. There were three teams out of Canada; that's why Budweiser called it the Budweiser International. Only five players from Tasty Pizza showed up at the civic center for the tournament that Saturday morning. The referee came over and told me that if I didn't put six on the ice in five minutes, he was going to call the game. I went over to Tom and told him to go out, play left wing, and stay away from everyone because if he got hurt, his mom would kill me. The players from Great Lakes Paper Co. were huge. Every one of them was over six feet, two inches tall. They showed up wearing hockey pants, shoulder pads, shin pads, and helmets. We only had kneepads, elbow pads, and gloves.

I told the team to hang back and play defense. I was hoping the rest of the team would show up quickly. It was near the end of the first period when it happened. I had a chance to go up and take a shot; I had one of the harder shots on the team, so I moved up and took my shot. It went wide, the goalie did not direct it to the corner, and it came off the backboard and straight out. Coming out of nowhere was Tom O'Brien. He took a shot, which went over the goalie's left shoulder and into the goal.

The announcer couldn't find Tom's number on the roster. There was a pause…

The announcer finally said, "Scoring for Tasty Pizza…" *Pause.* "Scoring for Tasty Pizza…" *Pause.* "The little guy!"

The crowd went wild! Tom got a standing ovation! It was unbelievable! Only God could orchestrate that. It gave Tom the confidence to conquer anything. After the period ended, we were up 1–0. When the rest of the team arrived before the start of the second period, they all wanted to know who scored the goal.

We answered, "Tom did."

Tasty Pizza Softball and Broomball team

At the start of the second period, all the jocks wanted to send Tom out to see if he could score again. After three periods of play, we ended up winning the game 2 to 1. We all still talk about that game years later. Tom never liked that story though. I think he resented the fact that he was smaller than the rest of us, and he didn't like being called the little guy. He found out going through life that you don't judge a book by its cover. It's what's inside that counts. He turned out to be a great husband, a great dad, a great person, and someone I am proud to call my friend. He is married now and has a beautiful wife, a beautiful home, and a beautiful daughter. She is a great hockey player. She gets it from her dad.

Think about what had to take place to make that all happen. I had to coach football, join Big Brothers Big Sisters of America, be the coach and manager of this broomball team, and buy Tom a complete uniform. Ronnie Kulas, who was getting married, had to have his stag party that Friday night before the game. Only five guys could show up that Saturday morning to start the game. Only God could put that altogether and make it happen.

As we got older, Tom, Mike, and I played on the same team. I played sports until I was fifty years old. I retired from the fire department and sports the same year. Tom and Mike became part of our family. Almost fifty years later, we still meet for lunch or dinner to keep in touch.

The war had such an impact on me, and so did the fact that I tested positive for Agent Orange, that herbicide they sprayed all over Vietnam. When we got married, we decided not to have children. After almost four years had passed, Peg stated she wanted children. I prayed for girls. If I had boys, I would never let them go off to war, and I didn't want to move to Canada. The good Lord answered my prayers and gave me two beautiful girls.

Kathleen Ann is my oldest. She graduated from Gustavus Adolphus College with honors. She spoke fluent Japanese and went to school in Osaka, Japan, for one year. Elizabeth Wells is my youngest. She also went to Gustavus Adolphus College and graduated with honors. She has a great job and lives in Eden Prairie in a beautiful three-bedroom, three-bathroom home with a big fenced-in backyard. All she needs now is a husband and lots of kids—grandkids for me. As life continued on, I realized God gave me not only two beautiful girls but also two young men that became part of our family.

CHAPTER 6

Out of the Service

1969

When I came home from Vietnam and purchased the double bungalow on Fifty-Fourth and James, Mom and I moved in together. It was pretty small on both sides but more than adequate for me. I had just spent the last thirteen months living in a tent. I even slept in a tree one night during the monsoons.

After living in that beautiful big home most of her life, I knew it had to be hard for Mom. She never said anything or ever complained. I think she felt she was still taking care of me, but the rules were now reversed. I think the good Lord helped me get the loan to buy the house so I could keep my promise to my father.

I met Peg—Margaret Elizabeth Sherman—at a party in South Minneapolis. Kevin Engelbretson was hosting a going-away party for his brother who was going into the Marine Corps. I was introduced to Peg, and we seemed to hit it off because we sat and talked for about an hour. Then she excused herself to go upstairs to the restroom and did not come back for a long time. After a half hour or so had passed and she still had not returned, I went to investigate. When I got upstairs, I found the bathroom door handle laying on the floor. When she grabbed the door handle to leave the bathroom, it had come right out. She was trapped in the bathroom! I picked up the handle, slid the square piece back in the square opening, and turned the knob, and the door opened. She thanked me for rescuing her, and we have been together since. I truly believe I was meant to meet her that night. God made the handle come out so I would go up and rescue her. It was meant to be.

I had just bought a house, was working two jobs, and had promised my father I would take care of my mom. I felt like I had way too much on my plate to get married and start a family. I was having nightmares of Vietnam way too often. When I would have a bad nightmare, I would be out for the rest of the night. I had four years of free college for serving in the military, but I had no idea how I could make that work. I was getting only four hours of sleep a night, and I couldn't take on anything else. Luckily, in 1972, I came to my senses. I realized that this young lady was my soulmate, and I couldn't live without her.

We had spent two years together before I proposed to her. At that time, her mother was dying of cancer and had very little time left. Her last dying wish was to come to the wedding of her daughter. We decided to get married in one week. In Minnesota, you have to have a marriage license for seven days before you get married. We had the marriage license, so all we needed was a church and a priest. Mrs. Sherman was a devoted Catholic and had helped out at least two days a week and every Sunday at the church.

Peg and I went to the Catholic Church to talk to the senior priest. We sat down and told him our situation. I told him that Mrs. Sherman had dedicated her life to the church. She helped out once or twice during the week and every Sunday. He responded that because I wasn't a devoted Catholic, I would have to go through so many weeks of schooling and become a Catholic before I could get married in the church. I told him that Mrs. Sherman might not last that long, that this was her last dying wish, and that he had an obligation to grant that wish. He explained that those were the rules of the church and there was nothing he could do. I told Peg that this was ridiculous and we were not going to sit there and listen any longer. As we walked out of the church, Peg started to cry.

Being a Marine, you learn to never give up: You adapt, improvise, overcome, and complete the mission. When we got back home, I called a friend and told him our situation. He was a pastor, but I told him I needed a priest and a Catholic Church. He told me to give him an hour, and he'd call me back. He found a priest and a Catholic Church in Fridley, Minnesota. The wedding was on.

We got married on August 8, 1972. It was a hot day, and there was no air conditioning in the church. None of that seem to matter though. Father Tim asked how long I wanted to make the ceremony. I replied that Mrs. Sherman was in the wheelchair in the center aisle and that he should keep an eye on her. If she was doing well, go with it; if she began to look like she was failing, cut it short.

The wedding turned out great. We didn't have a thousand people or anything like that, but it wasn't about the guests. We were happy, and we granted Peg's mom her last dying wish. She passed away just a few weeks after that. Just as I knew he would, even though things looked bad, the good Lord intervened and found us a priest and a church. We all take many things that happen in our life for granted. I truly believe God saved me in Vietnam because he had a plan for me. Not knowing what that was, I just walked down the path where he led me.

In a year and a half, Peg and I will spend our fiftieth wedding anniversary together. We never went anywhere when we got married because we got married with a week's notice, and I had no vacation time and couldn't get off work. Maybe on our fiftieth wedding anniversary, we will take that wonderful vacation. We will see what God has planned for us.

We spent four years and five months together before we had children. When Kathleen Ann arrived on January 11, 1977, we talked about moving into a bigger home. We found a little piece of land in Eden Prairie and built the new home. It wasn't a fancy big home, but we loved it. The house was a split-level, and only the upper half was finished. I spent the next ten years finishing the lower level and doing the landscaping.

My neighbor, Jerry Miller, built his home with his own two hands over five years while working at WCCO. He was an electrical engineer, and if I ever needed help or advice, he was always there. Over the years, Jerry became my best friend. We would debate everything and anything. Most importantly, at the end of the day, we would agree to disagree.

Jerry and Dee, his wife, took Peg and me out to dinner one night. I will never forget that night. Jerry informed us that he was diagnosed with Lou Gehrig's disease. He explained that there were two types. One affected the upper part of the body, and the other affected the lower portion of the body. Jerry told us he only had a little over a year to live. I was shocked and couldn't believe it. I thought everything was going to be fine. Within six months, Jerry was in a wheelchair. I mowed his lawn all summer, raked his leaves all fall, and shoveled his driveway all winter. Dee had a hard time getting Jerry in and out of the car, so I drove Jerry to all his doctor's appointments. Jim, their son, came over and got me the night Jerry passed away in their home. It was like losing a brother. Jerry told me once that friends sometimes treat you better than family. Eventually, Jim got married, and Dee moved into a smaller house. I think of him often and couldn't have asked for a better friend.

CHAPTER 7

I Joined the Eden Prairie Fire Department

After living in Eden Prairie for about three years, I was traveling east on Valley View Road just before Graffiti Bridge. I came across a house fire. The supply line from the hydrant to the fire truck went across the road. I got out of my car to watch the firemen work. As they dragged the hose up to the house to put out the fire, one of the firemen came back to the truck to get another hose. As he pulled the hose off the truck, it got all tangled up. He was having trouble straightening it out, so I went over to help. Then I helped him drag it up to the house. When the fire was out, they started to remove the hose across the road. A fireman came over, handed me his card, and told me to be at the central fire station at 5:00 p.m. the next day because he was going to sign me up. I got that feeling all over again. It was a good Lord speaking to me, and I knew what I had to do. I would be there at 5:00 p.m.

Later, I found out that fireman was Jack Hackett, the director of public safety for Eden Prairie. I had no idea what I was getting myself into, but I knew I had to do it. I had made that promise to the good Lord, and I believed the day I did not comply with his wishes, he would dial up my number.

Bob Grant, Firefighter; Eden Prairie, MN

The fire department ended up being one of the most rewarding things I ever did. You cannot imagine pulling someone out of a wrecked car or a burning building and just being part of that. It was very rewarding. I remember Curt Oberlander coming out of a burning house carrying a dog and then doing mouth-to-mouth on the dog because it was overcome by smoke. He saved the dog. I gave him doggy breath spray for Christmas that year. The owners of that dog brought a cake, brownies, and cookies to our central fire station the next time we had training. They could not thank us enough for saving their dog's life, even though the house was a total loss.

To become a fireman, you must attend many weeks of vo-tech school. I took every class the fire department offered. I even became an EMT, an emergency medical technician. This required a state license that was renewed every year. I took structural classes, fairground command classes, and classes to become a driver operator. One course that was a lot of fun was the high-speed pursuit school for state troopers. All firemen who wanted to become driver operators had to go through this class, which was held in St. Cloud, Minnesota.

The state troopers really knew what they were doing, and they were great teachers. The driving course was sprayed with water to make it very slippery. We started our training in a police car. The trooper sat in the right front seat and had two pedals on the floor. The right pedal locked up the right front brake. The left pedal locked up the left front brake. As we drove down the scores, we would see cones out in front of us. One would be out to the right; the next one would be ten yards down to the left. When we started to go around the right cone, the trooper would tap that right pedal and send us into a slide. We would have to make adjustments to get out of the slide and try and make it around the cone. After maneuvering through the course in the police car, we moved up to a van, a small school bus, and finally, the large school bus.

I had never been in a slide driving a large school bus. I learned a lot that day, thanks to the technical training of the state troopers. The one vehicle I drove the most on the fire department was our aerial ladder. I think if everyone had an opportunity to go through this course, we would all be better drivers.

Being a fireman, the more classes you took, the more information you could collect, and the hands-on, everyday experience made you a better fireman. Every time the tones went off at the station or your pager beeped on your belt, you had no idea what you are getting into. For example, once, my pager went off at 4:00 a.m. The call came across as a possible car fire, which was pretty routine stuff; nothing to get your heart racing. I lived on Top View Road, one of the higher spots in Eden Prairie. When I reached Top View Road and Roberts Drive, just two blocks from my house, I could see flames three hundred feet in the air. *Car fire my six!* My heart rate jumped, the adrenaline kicked in, and I pushed a little harder on the gas pedal.

I was always the first one in the door for a call in the middle of the night. When I got to the station, Tom Montgomery, the station captain, was already there. I asked how he beat me. He told me that whatever it was, when it blew, it rocked his house. I was driving as five firemen jumped on engine two out of station two. We were the closest to the accident. As we passed Eden Prairie Center, the road dipped down and then back up a slight incline. We could see the flames covering the entire roadway—a three hundred-foot wall of flames. I put my left turn signal on and was going to make the loop around and come in from the other side. Just then, the officer on the scene told us there was a man trapped in the fire, and we didn't have time to go around. The left side of the highway was open, and we were supposed to come on through there.

Tom Montgomery, sitting in the office seat, said that we were going through. Being a good Marine, I knew the importance of following orders. I took the engine out of first gear, shifted into second, and headed toward the wall of flames.

When we passed through the wall of flames, we could see a large tanker truck laying on its side. He had been carrying six thousand gallons of gasoline. When he rolled the truck, the tank ruptured, and the sparks ignited the gas.

We made a quick U-turn, tagged the hydrant, and started pulling lines. We knew we wouldn't have enough foam on the truck to put this fire out. We called the central station and asked for a fifty-five-gallon drum of foam.

There was a true hero that day, and it wasn't one of us. At every house fire, apartment fire, or any type of structural fire, there was always a fireman that ran into the fire to rescue the individual. That day it was a passerby. Driving his pickup truck on his way to work, this guy came across the tanker truck on fire, took a mattress out the back of his pickup, used it as a shield, and walked into this fire to pull the driver out. The driver of the tanker truck had burns over 99 percent of his body. If there was ever a time God was watching over someone, he was watching over those two men that day, not only the passerby that went in and rescued the driver, but the driver himself.

The driver was placed in an ambulance and headed to HCMC. The doctors found a small patch of skin under his belt buckle. They needed a piece of unburned skin so they could grow new skin that his body would not reject. Nine months later, that man walked out of the hospital. The true hero that day was that passerby that risked his life to save someone he didn't even know.

During my years on the fire department, I believe I had an impact on many lives. If you have ever been part of saving a life, you will know what I mean. There is nothing more rewarding.

I was driving to a call on Highway 169 close to the Lions Tap. Between the Lions Tap and the top of the hill by the airport, we averaged seven deaths a year. Whenever we got a call on that stretch of roadway, we knew it was going to be bad. The roadway was icy, and the lady was headed up the hill. As the road turned slightly to the left, she slid straight ahead, turning her wheels more. When she hit dry pavement, her car scooted across the highway and hit a semi head on. The semitruck never had a chance to touch his brakes. They were each traveling at about fifty miles an hour. The impact was so violent that it flipped the semi on its side.

Engine two was first on the scene. I was driving, Tim Sather was the officer, and we had three experienced firemen in the back. The car looked like an accordion. The one victim in the car was the woman driving it. We immediately called for air rescue, a chopper out of Hennepin County Medical Center. We set up an LZ, *a landing zone*. By the time the chopper arrived, we had cut the roof off the car, cut the steering column, and cut away the metal that had her leg trapped. When we got her to the chopper and she was lifting off, the state trooper standing next to me asked me how old I thought she was. I guessed thirty to forty. The trooper told me she was sixteen and had just got her license. With all the trauma she had, I didn't think she had a chance. But we always did our best, not knowing what the good Lord had in store for them. I found out later that she made it. The state troopers used her car at the state fair for many years with the big sign next to the car: Seat Belts Save Lives.

Once I responded to a car accident involving two cars. The first car had a single male around fifty years old. The second had a father and daughter; the young girl was around twelve and the father about thirty years old. As we pulled the fifty-year-old male out of the first car, we could all smell alcohol. Witnesses said the first car drifted across the centerline and hit the second car head on. The young girl was pronounced dead on the scene. Captain Jim Clark of the Eden Prairie Police was in charge. He came over to me and told me to go over and stay by the father because if he realized what had happened, he might try to kill the drunk driver. My job was to see that didn't happen. I did what Jim asked, but in the back of my mind, I wanted to help the dad go beat on that drunk. When I would come home from bad calls, my wife could always tell I was affected by it. She was always very good at not prying or asking about the call. I truly thank her for that.

Near the end of my career as a fireman, I looked back and thought maybe this was why the good Lord spared me that night of the Tet Offensive in Vietnam.

As a fireman, you miss many holidays, birthdays, special events, and even Christmas morning. We got a call about 4:00 a.m. one Christmas morning. It was a house fire. On the way to the call, I was thinking how sad it was, that I hoped they didn't have children, and that I hoped everyone got out safely. When we arrived on the scene, we found out everyone was safe. The house was well engulfed in fire, and we had our work cut out for us. It's even more difficult when you have to deal with snow and ice.

We extinguished the flames, but the house was not livable. The family went to a nearby hotel. They had two young children, and all their presents were burnt up in the fire. One of the Eden Prairie firemen made a call to a friend that owned a toy store. He agreed to open up the store. We all chipped in money and went over and bought presents for the kids.

When I got home that day, my two daughters Katie and Betsy seemed upset with me because it was now 10:00 a.m., and Mom made them wait to open presents. I made them go get on their coats, mittens, and hats and get in the car. We drove over to that house that was badly burned. It was only a few blocks away.

When I stopped in front of the house, I asked Katie what was laying in the front yard. She paused for a minute, then she said, "The Christmas tree."

I said, "You're right. How lucky are we? *We* are going home to our little house to have Christmas."

On the way back to the house, I told them how all the firemen got together, chipped in money, and bought presents for the little kids. When we got back to the house, little did I know the two of them got together and made a plan. When under the tree each got a present, they wanted to give it to the children. Sometimes you can turn a tragedy into a great learning experience. I was never as proud of my two daughters as I was that day. As I said many times in this book, the good Lord was leading me down this path.

At dinner that day, we said grace and a prayer for that family. We were thankful that all got out safe, and that was the only thing that really mattered. Elizabeth rode the school bus for a few years with one of the children from that fire. They became friends, but she did not know who he was. Years later after college when Elizabeth was attending Grace Church, they met again. They even dated for a while, but it wasn't meant to be.

STATE OF MINNESOTA
EXECUTIVE DEPARTMENT

ARNE H. CARLSON
Governor of the State of Minnesota

N O T I C E   O F   A P P O I N T M E N T

ROBERT GRANT

7203 Topview Road
Eden Prairie, Minnesota 55346

County of Hennepin

Congressional District Three

Because of the special trust and confidence I have in your integrity, judgment and ability, I have appointed and commissioned you to have and to hold the said office of:

MEMBER REPRESENTING VOLUNTEER FIREFIGHTERS EMERGENCY RESPONSE COMMISSION

Effective: May 18, 1993

Expiring: First Monday in January, 1997

This appointment carries with it all rights, powers, duties, and emoluments granted by law and pertaining to this position until this appointment is superseded or annulled by me or other lawful authority or by any law of this State.

IN TESTIMONY WHEREOF, I have hereunto set my hand and caused the Great Seal of the State of Minnesota to be affixed at the Capitol in the City of Saint Paul, May 13, 1993.

Governor

Secretary of State

Replacing: John Senior

While on the Eden Prairie Fire Department, I got involved with two other organizations. The first was the Emergency Response

Commission. It was headed up by Jim Franklin under Governor Arne Carlson. We met at the capitol once a month. The commission was responsible for overseeing the investigation of any illegal pollution or chemical dumping in our rivers or streams. Our job was to investigate and determine if any laws have been broken.

If a corporation had dumped chemicals into a river, the commission would determine what the chemical was and how much was dumped into the river. Was it an accident, and if so, did they report it? That would determine the amount of the fine handed out to the corporation. Companies that dump chemicals on the ground, into rivers and streams, or into the air cause problems that affect all of us. In many cases, they don't report anything, and they think they can get away with that. When caught, the commission would fine those companies millions of dollars.

The ERC would also oversee all major disasters like tornadoes or hurricanes. I was appointed to a four-year term, and I am truly thankful for having the opportunity to learn and serve on the ERC.

The chief of Eden Prairie Fire at that time was Spence Conrad. He came to tell me that we were starting something new called citizens emergency response teams or CERT. Each team leader would be trained in many different areas in case of a major disaster that destroyed local police and fire, leaving no one to respond. The goal was to have a CERT team in every neighborhood. Each team was made up of ten to fifteen members. They would check damaged homes for survivors, mark the home once it was checked, and if it seemed unstable, mark it as such. The members were trained in basic medical assistance. Each member would receive a backpack full of things that would help during an emergency. The city of Eden Prairie had a CERT director who set up the instructors and the classes. This reminded me of my childhood. In the neighborhood I grew up in, everyone knew each other. They would get together many times throughout the year. That's something I don't see happening much anymore.

CHAPTER 8

Eden Prairie Police and Fire Department

Safety Camp

One of the officers on the Eden Prairie Fire Department was Curt Oberlander. He was also a police officer, and he started a three-day safety camp for seven- to nine-year-olds. They were taught many different aspects of safety: fire safety, stranger danger and being aware of strangers, water safety, electrical safety, drug and alcohol awareness, bicycle safety, stop, drop, and roll, and reporting a crime. Each team had an adult team leader and two helpers. There would be five teams that would rotate from class to class. Each class was about twenty kids. This was all set up outside at Round Lake Park.

Safety Camp; Kyle, 3rd grade, Summer 1996; Bob retired May 14, 1996

Because I worked for Lund Food Holdings for thirty-four years, I became friends with many of the vendors. The Häagen-Dazs rep was a good friend. I asked him if Häagen-Dazs wanted to get involved with Eden Prairie Police, Eden Prairie Fire, and Eden Prairie Park and Recreation and help with safety camp. Häagen-Dazs was more than happy to help. At the end of the three-day camp, all the kids received a medallion hung around their necks and a safety camp certificate of completion. Häagen-Dazs showed up at the ceremony with freezer carts full of ice cream bars. There always were bars left over. I couldn't thank them enough for their generosity. It was a big hit with both the kids and the adults.

Another company that got involved was Kemps. Mike Nentl donated orange juice and milk for snacks and lunch and ice cream for the ice cream social. Dennis Gustner from Oak Grove Dairy, Inc. donated orange juice, Tom A. Klaers from Edy's Ice Cream donated ice cream, and Michelle Limesand from Fist Brokerage Company donated Minute Maid Juice. We were served pizza every day for lunch. My brother-in-law Michael Myhre, part owner of a candy company, donated a lot of candy that we used to reward the kids who raised their hands and participated in each class. It took a lot of people to make safety camp work. All the firemen there were on their own time.

My youngest, Elizabeth, went to safety camp, and Katie, my oldest, was a helper. I still run into young men and women who attended safety camp. They told me how much fun they had and that they were glad it was still going on. What a tribute to Mr. Oberlander. He must be very proud.

CHAPTER 9

Eden Prairie Fire Department
Historical Department

1990–2000

Near the end of my career as a fireman, I started the historical department. Jack Hacking was retired, but he told me of an idea he had to place an 8 x 10 photo of each fireman on the wall at our central fire station. I went to the chief, Spence Conrad, for approval and funds for the project. He said there was no money available, but I didn't give up. I kept trying. I started making progress when I talked to the new director of public safety, Jim Clark. He was not only the director of public safety but also the chief of police and a true community leader. Additionally, he was a friend and a great softball player. After telling Jim my idea, he told me we would find the money someplace and gave the project his blessing.

To get a picture on the wall, firefighters had to meet the criteria of the relief association. They must have been on the department for ten years and in good standing. At that point, their picture went on the wall. I started taking pictures of everyone that met the criteria. I remember at our summer picnic that they came down one at a time, put on their fire gear, and stood next to the truck. I was missing only the one fireman who had been killed on a Boy Scout camping trip during a storm when a tree fell on his tent.

There were a few people helping me with the historical department. One was Rick Hammerschmidt. He took the individuals' pictures that were not in fire uniforms and cropped them into existing pictures. They looked so perfect that I couldn't tell. Rick was a big help—thank you, Rick! Another person that helped was Al Hansen. He was very talented with computers, and any time I needed help, I turned to Al. He helped a lot—thanks, Al!

Bonnie Riegert was the wife of a battalion chief, Stan Riegert. Bonnie collected and saved every newspaper article about the Eden Prairie Fire Department. She had close to a thousand articles collected over many years, and she allowed me access to all of them. I promised not to fold them or damage them in any way. I scanned them onto the computer, then edited and cropped them into files, which I organized by year. Each year with a major event that was on the front page of the paper was put on the wall in an 8 x 10 frame. The pictures start with the first chief, the first fire truck, and the first station.

When the department first started, this group of men had a chief and a fire truck but no station. One of the firemen that lived in the central part of the city kept the fire truck at his house. When a call came in, the wife of that individual started calling the other wives. Each one in turn would call another five. That's how the word got out back then. One summer's day, there was a call. As the firemen received the calls, they jumped in their cars and drove to the fire. The fireman that had the fire truck at his house was supposed to bring the truck. Time passed—and no truck. All of a sudden, the chief realized the person that had the truck was out of town. The substitute truck driver forgot he had the truck and drove to the scene.

It is stories like this that show the importance of the historical department. Many of the stories never made it to the front page of the paper. There are over one hundred 8 x 10 frames full of stories on the wall of the central fire department. If you ever get a chance, bring your kids to the Eden Prairie Fire Department open house. It's a lot of fun for the kids, and you can read some of the great stories.

Another idea I had was to start an Honorary Fire Chief award to disabled children. Bring them to the station, make them chief for a day, and give them a framed certificate and a real fire chief helmet—not some plastic thing that will get tossed away. I truly believe we could find some corporate entity that would sponsor this, so it wouldn't cost the city of Eden Prairie a dime. I presented this to the new fire chief in 2020. I hope he follows through on it.

Someone asked me after I retired if I missed it. I don't think I miss getting up at night, working all night on a house fire, and going to work the next morning. Many days I got no sleep. When it happened two or three nights in a row, it was hard on the body. In Vietnam I could easily go two or three days without sleep. When I came home from Vietnam, I could easily function on four hours of sleep. That was more than enough. I will always miss all the guys and gals on the department. The fire department has a picnic every year for the active firefighters and all the retirees. I try and make it, so I can see all my old friends.

Here is a picture of me when I became Fire Fighter of the Year 1995.

There is one fireman who I became good friends with that, for some reason, thinks that I saved his life. I didn't. I was just doing my job. Every time he sees me, he asks me how he looks, and we both start to laugh. He was riding his motorcycle on Prairie Center Drive when he came up to Highway 169 where they had just put in a new stoplight. He saw a semitruck slowing, and he was going to stop at the intersection. The light was green, so he went to cross Highway 169. A very elderly woman in the right lane next to the semi never saw the red light. She was traveling at fifty miles per hour. When Gary cleared the front of the semi, he never saw her coming. She hit him broadside at fifty miles an hour. I was at the station washing my car when the call came in. We were two blocks away. One other fireman had just stopped by. Since we were both EMTs, we jumped in the ambulance and headed that way.

Gary was hurt very badly. The right side of his body was mangled, and he'd slid down the pavement on his face. He was losing a lot of blood, so we put on the mast trousers, which take the blood out of the lower extremities. When you do this, many times the patient will regain consciousness. At the time, I had no idea who my patient was. As we were getting ready to put him on the stretcher, Gary suddenly opened his eyes. He recognized me and asked, "BeeGee, how do I look?" I recognized his voice and realized who he was.

Remember the movie *Papillion* where he sticks his head out that door and the person next to him who looked like death says, "How do I look?"

Papillion says, "GOOD! GOOD! YOU LOOK GOOD!"

That's what popped into my head. I said to Gary, "GOOD! GOOD! YOU LOOK GOOD!"

Gary and I get together once or twice a year. He will always be a good friend.

CHAPTER 10

Becoming a Shriner

Some members of the Grant family would get together once a month and for dinner. My cousin, Richard Grant Sr., had been a longtime member of the Shriners organization. I told him I seemed to have a lot of time on my hands since I retired from the fire department. My cousin suggested that I should become a Shriner. Sitting at the table, it all happened again. I got that rush through my body and broke out in sweat, and my heart rate went way up. I knew right then I was supposed to be a Shriner. I had no idea what that meant or what I had to do to become a Shriner. The one thing I can tell you is that everything about the Shriners' organization is very secretive. You take an oath never to divulge anything about the Shriners' organization.

After becoming a Shriner, I visited the Shriners Children's Hospital. That is a day I'll never forget. I had my fez hat on; that's the headgear that all Shriners wear. It wasn't the parents coming up and thanking us for saving their child's life as much as it was the smiles on all the children's faces that made me feel good. What a great organization! Over a million children have come through those doors to be treated, and their parents never had to pay a dime. I am proud to be part of this organization. I can truly see why the good Lord would want me to get involved.

The children in this hospital and the children in the middle of Vietnam…when I looked at them, here and there…all I saw was pure innocence. All the hate that they acquired throughout their lives we taught them. To know what pure innocence is, just pick up babies. Look into their eyes, the gateway to their souls. Even in the middle of Vietnam, when we went into a village and looked into the eyes of small children, we could tell if their hearts were filled with love or hate. If we would stop teaching and preaching hate, this world would be a much better place.

I had a flashback the other day. You never know what will cause them or why they happen. The only thing I've come up with is that God causes those flashbacks. Why? I believe he is reminding me how bad it was in Vietnam and of the promise I made to him that night during the Tet Offensive. It is all part of a plan to keep me on the straight and narrow and heading down his path.

CHAPTER 11

Veteran Memorial Committee

Eden Prairie Veterans Memorial

1995–2002

My daughter, Elizabeth Wells Grant, was on the arts and crafts commission for Eden Prairie. There was a group of individuals that got together to build a veterans' memorial. They needed someone to be the liaison between the city and the committee. Elizabeth volunteered for the job. After learning about the veterans' memorial, she called me.

"Dad," she said. "There's a committee you have to join. It's the Eden Prairie Veterans' Memorial Committee."

Eden Prairie Veterans memorial, E.P.V.M.C.

Yes, you're right—it happened all over again. God had another plan for me, and I needed to become part of this committee. The committee was made up of old and young, male and female, military and nonmilitary. They were all dedicated to one thing: building a veterans' memorial. After being approved by the city to move forward, we were given three pieces of property to choose from. Our final choice was Purgatory Creek Recreational Area. We were not fond of the name, but the city would not change it. The area was about 50 percent wetlands with a pond that had a water fountain just off the shore. Our original budget was $300,000. A group of individuals who had built a memorial in Northfield, Minnesota met with us to give us some insight into building a memorial. They were very helpful. They told us whatever our budget was to double it. We stayed with $300,000.

Our plan consisted of two intertwining circles. In the middle of each circle would be a bronze sculpture. The first circle had a Marine carrying an injured pilot over his shoulder; etched in granite around them were the words *All gave some, but some gave all*. The second circle had a nurse with her hand on a world globe; etched in granite around her were the words *Imagine world peace*. Around each circle was a 2 1/2 foot granite wall etched with famous quotations from history. There was an entrance to the memorial from all four sides; however, the main entrance had three flagpoles. The middle and highest was the American flag. On one side was the Minnesota flag, and on the other was a POW flag. There were walls on each side of the entryway. Etched in granite on the right side were all the KIAs—killed in action.

One of the committee members, Richard Fay, had a son killed in action. I was skeptical about faces being etched in granite because I did not know how they would turn out. When Richard Fay told me that the image looked exactly like his son, I was thrilled. Under each portrait was the name of the soldier, his branch of service, and the conflict that he served in. The letters K-I-A stand at the end. Etched in granite on the left side of the entryway were the names of the committee members and anyone else who wanted their name on the memorial. For $250, someone could put their name, branch of service, and the conflict that he served in. That can still be done today (2020), but the price has gone up to $300.

Our original budget of $300,000 only covered cement walls with bronze plaques. We went to the office of Ed Flaherty. We understood he was interested in donating to the memorial. He asked me when I served in Vietnam and where. He told us he lost five good friends in Vietnam during that same period. I felt like I had a connection with him; I could see in his eyes he truly understood. We talked for about an hour, then he opened his checkbook and wrote out a check for $100,000. His only request was to make it matchup money. For every dollar we collected, he would match it up to $100,000. He also told us that he had connections with the granite company in St. Cloud. That's when our plans changed from cement to granite.

The next time our budget went up was when we met with Neil Brodin, the individual we chose to do our sculptures. The committee from Northfield that came up to help us thought the sculptures would be about $50,000 each. Mr. Brodin informed us it would be $100,000 for each person in each statue. The sculpture of the Marine carrying the Navy pilot actually contained two people—two sculptures! We now had over $300,000 for bronze sculptures, which put our budget at about $600,000. That put me back on my heels a bit. Knowing it would be difficult to raise $600,000, I never said anything. I don't know what the other committee members were thinking, but we all moved forward with the project.

E.P. Veterans Memorial

Everyone on the committee worked very hard. It took up a lot of my time. I tried to call on as many corporate headquarters as I could each day. I wouldn't talk to any secretaries, vice presidents, or presidents—only the CEOs. Two things I had going for me were that I had been there and done this, and I wasn't selling a dead horse. Walmart donated $50,000, and with Ed Flaherty's $100,000 matching money, many of the corporations in Eden Prairie understood the memorial was going to happen and also donated money.

Even before the memorial was finished, after the groundbreaking we met at the memorial site once a year to celebrate Memorial Day. We always honored three veterans who had a connection to Eden Prairie. The names of these individuals would be nominated by friends and family. The committee would then choose the three to be honored that year. In the early years, the committee voted to honor me. I declined. I told them there were 58,000 men that didn't come home from Vietnam, and they had to honor each and every one of them before I might consider it.

I asked a friend named Tim Sather to join the committee. Tim was a Marine in Vietnam the same time I was. He was shot twice and still survived. I got to know him on the Eden Prairie Fire Department. We responded to the same station and rode in the same truck together many times. That year we honored Tim in place of me. All the men and women I met over the years that we honored on Memorial Day are true heroes, and they always will be.

The NFL players, instead of taking a knee at the beginning of each game and disgracing the American flag, should stand tall, place one of those heroes at midfield, and have him tell his story. I have no doubt that individual would get a standing ovation. Do you know how many people have served this country in the military? It is over forty million people. For every person who served, at least ten more people are connected to that person. When you take a knee, you now have offended 400 million people. Keep taking a knee, and I guarantee you there will be a big impact at the box office.

I would like to tell you about a few individuals we honored on Memorial Day. The first is a young Marine named Joe Piram, who served two tours in Iraq and one in Afghanistan. Joe and his team were hit by an IED. Some of his comrades survived that explosion. They received care at ABAMC in San Antonio, Texas. Joe was burned over 60 percent of his body. Did he give up or quit? No. After many months of treatment and rehabilitation, he came home to Eden Prairie. I first met him at a fundraiser at the Chanhassen American Legion. He became a reserve officer on the Eden Prairie Police Department, finished law enforcement training, became a police officer in Edina, and joined the Eden Prairie Veterans' Memorial Committee. Joe Piram, like everyone we honored, is a hero.

The next individual I would like to tell you about is Major Woodrow G. Franklin. He enlisted in the Marines and served in Vietnam from October 1965 to October 1967. He rose through the ranks to E-7 gunnery sergeant. He was selected to receive the rank of chief warrant officer. When he retired, he had reached the rank of major. I first met him when he was an Eden Prairie Police reserve officer. He would show up every year at our memorial service. He and two other reserve officers would post and retire the American flag, the Minnesota flag, and the POW flag.

The next individual is Capt. Arvin R. Chauncy. He was awarded his naval aviator wings in March 1957 and began flying combat missions in the A-4 in February 1967. He flew fifty-seven missions over Vietnam. He was shot down by enemy aircraft fire, captured, and spent the next 2,104 days as a prisoner of war of the North Vietnamese. He was repatriated during Operation Homecoming on March 4, 1973, and returned to flight status. He served thirty-one years in active duty and received two Silver Star Citation awards. His final assignment was as commanding officer at the Navy ROTC unit at the University of Minnesota. I met with him for lunch where we talked about honoring him at our memorial. I was truly moved by his story. If there was ever someone to look up to and consider as role model for children, this is your man. He is truly an American hero.

These are just a few of the stories that should be on the six o'clock news every night. These are the stories that would lift us up, make us proud, and make America feel good about itself again. I know God would be proud, and so would I. We have to stop putting people on pedestals that don't belong there. My son-in-law won't allow his children to watch television because there is too much violence and hate. We turn on the news, and all we see are demonstrations in the street, looting and burning. Our politicians cannot get it right. They forgot why they are there. We have to start believing in this country again.

CHAPTER 12

Suicide

2004

There is one thing in my life I am not proud of. It was a dark time in my life when I was not dealing with things very well. I had nightmares almost every day, and I decided to end it all. I was transported to Hennepin County Medical Center. After three weeks there, I was ordered to go the VA for treatment where I spent fourteen weeks under the care of Dr. Charles Peterson. I can't thank him enough for all that he did for me.

While I was at the VA in Minneapolis, the veterans would get together in groups headed up by Dr. Peterson. When it came their turn, each person in the group was supposed to talk about something that was bothering them. Whenever it was my turn, I would pass. I did not want to talk about anything. I met a young Marine about my age who was in Vietnam during the Tet Offensive. His dad owned one thousand acres in South Dakota. He lived in a tent on his dad's farm with a big lake stocked with fish and woods full of deer. After many weeks, he came to me and told me that if I ever needed a place to stay, he had room in his tent. I think about him now and then and hope that his dad helped him get back on track.

Rick Hall, who was in my bunker the night of the Tet Offensive, lived in his dad's basement for two years. We would talk on the phone now and then. Rick must have told his dad about me because one day his dad called me. After talking with me for over an hour, he asked if he could come and see me. Sure. He flew to Minneapolis, and we spent an afternoon together. He asked me why I wasn't affected in the same way as his son. I told him I was struggling with nightmares but was trying to hold it together because of the promise I made to my father that I would take care of my mom. I knew he was very well to do. I told him to drag his son out of the basement, take him to work, and give him a job. Even if it was a job he was no good at it, make sure he got up and went to work every day—no more free ride in the basement. That's just what he did, and Rick is now married and has a family. I think the one thing that saved me was that I didn't have time to feel sorry for myself. I had too much on my plate and promises to keep.

The US Department of Veterans Affairs released a study that showed from 2009 to 2010, roughly twenty-two veterans were dying by suicide every day. That is one every sixty-five minutes. In 2011, that number climbed to twenty-three every day. In 2018, there were 325 active-duty suicides. Marines took their lives at 150 percent of the rate of those serving in the Navy and Army. If you know someone who might be in trouble, reach out to them.

CHAPTER 13

Evelyn Hansen—the Miracle Baby

The next time the good Lord spoke to me, it hit closer to home. My oldest daughter, Katie, was having her third child. She had two healthy boys prior to that. William was the older, and Isaac was the younger.

When she was four months pregnant, she had a checkup. The doctor wanted to run a few tests, one of those being an amniocentesis. The result of that test showed there was a problem. One of the baby's genetic markers was not connected. The doctors knew if any marker from twenty down is not connected, then the outcome will be bad. For example, if number 18 is not connected, the child will have Down syndrome. From marker number 10 down, the child cannot live.

Katie's baby's number 10 genetic marker was not connected. The doctors told Matt and Katie that their baby's diagnosis was terminal and she would probably die in the womb. If she was born, she might survive for a couple hours or a couple days. The doctors' recommendation was to abort the child.

Matt and Katie, being very religious, told the doctors that if God wanted their child, God would take the baby. The next five months after, the diagnosis were very stressful for Matt and Katie. They asked the doctors for more information about what exactly was wrong with their child. The doctor told them that one kidney had failed and would have to be removed the day she was born, and that they didn't believe that she would live through that surgery. She would be born with no rectum, which would require creating a new one and redoing all the plumbing. This surgery would have to be done within the first twenty-four hours after birth. The doctors didn't believe she could possibly live through those two surgeries. Additionally, the baby had tumors on her lungs and in her brain and a cleft palate. She would require braces on her hands and feet, a respirator, and a feeding tube. She would be deaf and blind.

Katie carried her baby full-term. She and Matt welcomed their little girl, Evelyn Elizabeth Hansen, into the world on April 28, 2010. Elizabeth, Peg, and I were there that day. Matt's family lived in Chicago and was not able to attend, but we all knew their thoughts and prayers were with us.

When they brought the baby to meet us after the birth, I said, "Evelyn, it's your Grandpa. I love you."

She turned her head and looked right at me. I knew right then that she could hear a little and see a little. We did not know how much.

When Evelyn was born, the doctors found a hole in her right ear leaking brain fluid. She would need a bone, skin, and muscle graft to repair her right ear. Now there would be three big surgeries in a short period of time. Whenever Evelyn was taken for surgery, Matt went with her and stayed with her the whole time.

Matt and Katie came to us wondering if we would like to get a place together. I was newly retired and had just finished painting the inside and the outside of our home, putting down all new carpet, replacing our black-top driveway with cement, and installing two new garage doors. We had planned on spending the rest of our life in that house. Life was just starting! With the house paid in full, no credit card bills, and enough income to enjoy life and maybe travel a little or take a cruise, we were both ready for retirement.

After Peg and I talked it over, we decided that we could make it work.

Matt and I started looking on the Internet for a home large enough for seven. We also hoped for a little land to go with it. We found a place in Randolph, Minnesota, a small town just north of Northfield. When we went to look at it, it was empty. The bank had foreclosed on it over five years previously. It had broken doors and windows, and a lot of the copper had been torn out. We found a dead raccoon, a dead cat, and a live mouse in the bathtub, which had a big crack in it. With all the broken windows, there were Japanese beetles everywhere and millipedes all over the floor. The downside was that the house was in pretty rough shape. The upside was that it came with twenty acres and seven outbuildings, even though most of the outbuildings were in rough shape.

Matt looked at me and said, "This place has great potential!"

Peg and Katie almost fell over. "You're kidding, right?"

When we moved in, it was summer, and we had a lot to do before winter came. The house was a big old farmhouse with eight bedrooms and four bathrooms, but only one toilet worked. Because the one working toilet was on the upper level, we had to carry buckets of water upstairs to get it to flush. When the bank foreclosed on the previous owners, they shut everything down in the house, including the furnace. Part of the home was a new addition with in-floor heat. Instead of putting antifreeze in the lines in the cement, the owner at the time had put in water. The first winter all the lines froze. When we did a systems check, we found that not one line would hold pressure, so there was no heat in that half of the house.

Attached to the house was a two-car garage. I built a 3 x 5 room in the garage, insulated it from top to bottom, and installed a furnace. I then ran ductwork throughout the new addition. All the ductwork had to be framed and sheet rocked, which we hadn't counted on. A few other things happened that we hadn't counted on. The main furnace in the house failed. The well froze up, and the water heater failed. The previous owner had installed tile everywhere, but none of it matched. That all had to be removed before we could put down carpet. To this day, we still have a lot of work ahead of us. We are trying to keep our heads above water and take things one day at a time.

I have the utmost respect for Matt because he works ten-hour days, six days a week. After coming home from work and grabbing a bite, he works another three to four hours on the house. He does his best to be a good father, a good husband, a good provider, and a good friend. Sometimes I wonder how Katie and Matt have kept it together. The stress has to be overwhelming.

Evelyn Hansen

When little Evelyn came home from the hospital, I took a picture of her. Every time I look at it, she looks like a little angel. Peg and I tried to help anyway we could. Evelyn had to be fed every hour on the hour. There is no way Katie could stay up twenty-four hours a day, raise two boys, run a household, cook meals, and help Matt with the business. Peg and Katie took shifts. Peg would get up at three in the morning and take a shift so Katie could get some sleep. If Katie felt there was something wrong with Evelyn, she would come and get me. My EMT and the fire department experience were useful. Katie and I would take Evelyn to Northfield Hospital. The doctors there would take one look at her chart and tell us that Evelyn's situation was way above their expertise. Then they would place Evelyn and Katie in an ambulance and rush them to Children's Hospital in downtown Minneapolis. This happened over thirty times the first two years of Evelyn's life.

Dr. Dave Dassenko was chief of staff at Children's Hospital in downtown Minneapolis. When Evelyn and Katie arrived at Children's Hospital, Dr. Dassenko would meet them and take charge of her treatment. Our family can't thank Dr. Dassenko enough for all his care and compassion. Dr. Dassenko and his team of doctors and nurses are the best. We will always be indebted to them. There is a picture and a plaque of Evelyn Hansen at Children's Hospital that says *The Miracle Baby*.

Katie and Evelyn Hansen

When we found out four months into Katie's pregnancy that her baby might have a problem, the whole family, all my friends, and everyone at our church prayed for little Evelyn. If there is anyone out there who doesn't believe our Almighty God has the power to save lives, they should come and meet little Evelyn. They will become a believer.

This may be the end of my journey. I think Almighty God will keep me here as long as I can be helpful. I don't believe the good Lord has any other journey for me down the road. I also believe that death is not the end. Death is the beginning.

I know there are those who judge me poorly for not going to church. I believe I am more in tune and connected to God than most people on this planet. I am here because of God, and I have given myself to him unconditionally. I am doing my very best to keep my promise to him.

When I was pretty sick one day, my daughter Elizabeth wanted the family to hold hands and pray for me. I didn't feel comfortable with that, and I'll tell you why. When I asked the good Lord to save me the night of the Tet Offensive, he granted that prayer. He gave me the ultimate gift: the gift of life. After receiving that gift of life, I could never go back to ask or pray for more. If I am sick or in pain, it is what the good Lord wants. I have spent my entire life trying to keep that promise of being a good and productive member of society. I have listened every time he spoke to me and done my best to make him proud. I will only know how I did on Judgment Day. If God would tell me today that this is the day, I would not whine, cry, or ask for a few more hours or days. I would thank him for all the time he has given me. I meant no disrespect to Elizabeth that day, and I hope after she reads this that she will understand.

Here is a letter my daughter Katie wrote for a fund raiser for Evelyn:

CASTLE ROCK & ROLE BAR & GRILL
Seventh Annual Fundraiser for Evelyn Hansen
150 + mile Motorcycle run
Includes shirt, cinnamon rolls & coffee, food on
    route, and dinner after
At Castle Rock and Roll

Here is Katie's Story

With excessive amounts of not only morning sickness, but all day illness, I knew something just wasn't right with my pregnancy early on. However I turned down blood tests until my 20th week ultra sound. It was Christmas of 2009 when we were told our baby had *"unusual markers"* and needed to go see a specialist. The specialist found an irregular blood flow in the heart, a murmur, a brain tumor, an enlarged kidney, and other irregular measurements. Our baby had been diagnosed with Trisomy 10-P. The geneticist told us that this was one in a billon diagnosis. The doctors did not expect our baby to live past the second trimester. We were told our baby would be greatly deformed internally and externally, probably blind and deaf, and have seizures even if she did live. With devastation in our eyes, the geneticist offered us the option to abort the baby and end our suffering now. We immediately decided that if God wanted to have this baby, he would have taken it without us having a hand in it.

The baby was followed weekly at the perinatal clinic in Minneapolis. And weekly we were told that the baby would probably not live. The weeks passed, and with complications I went in for an emergency C-section at 38.5 weeks. Evelyn Elizabeth Hansen was born on April 28, 2010, in a room of 20 people or more, and then she was transferred to Children's Hospital. She weighed 6 lbs. 2 oz. Within the first few hours we were told of her missing anus, cleft palate, extremely enlarged kidney, and very low tone. She would not nurse or suck on a bottle, so she had surgery to implant a feeding tube into her stomach. Each time she was fed, she would vomit up her food. Her enlarged kidney was thought to be the cause. She remained in the N.I.C.U. for 31 days. Her strength at a minimum, they asked if I wanted to take her home. She would have frequent hospice meetings and probably won't live very long, so we they kept in touch. Evelyn's first year of life included so many visits to the hospital, several surgeries including having a G-tube in her stomach, her right kidney failure and removal, her J-Tube placed, and bi-lateral ear tubes resulting in the recovery from deafness in her right ear.

Fast forward to her first birthday, April 2011, and she still only weighed 13 pounds. The cleft palate repair wouldn't take place until she was at least 18 pounds. When her weight reached 19 pounds, the pallet was repaired in October 2011. I was excited because we saw a reduction in her gag reflex and her vomiting once the swelling subsided. She was able to keep more weight on and gain enough strength to remain sitting with a pillow behind her. The Doctor gave me the okay to try feeding her table food for the first time in December 2011. She was 20 months along. I had a great time teaching her to eat. She was able to keep herself upright in a high chair and have steady head control for the first time. She was eating up to 2 tablespoons of Gerber baby food three times a day by January 2012. Then late January brought a cold and even more vomiting again. By February 15th the vomit, which contained small blood flecks, suddenly burst into straight blood with clots the size of my thumbnail. After five days in the hospital with a biopsy, 20 days at home, and then back to the hospital with more bleeding and another biopsy in March, the results were inconclusive. In April 2012 Evelyn received the hearing aid to improve her partial hearing in her left ear and a bone conducted receiver in her right ear to help with localization. In May 2012 we were at home with no clear plans for the future, but we had day to day goals. We are working towards making our home handicap accessible. Traveling each day brings something new. Every day is a blessing.

There are not enough words to thank Tracy and Cheryl for putting this on. It took a great deal of work just to set this up, and a great deal of work to prepare all the food and serve it to everyone that showed up. From Matt, Katie, William, Isaac, Evelyn, Bob and Peg, we thank you from the bottom of our hearts.

CHAPTER 14

Footprints

Here is the story that I found on a bookmark that helped me understand how the good Lord watched over me:

One night, a man had a dream.

He determined he was walking along the beach with the Lord, and across the sky flashed scenes from his life. For each scene he noticed two sets of footprints in the sand. One belonged to him and the other to the Lord. When the last scene flashed before him, he looked back at the footprints in the sand. He noticed that many times along the path of his life, there was only one set of footprints. He also noticed that it happened at the very lowest and saddest times of his life. This really perplexed him, and he asked the Lord about it. "Lord, you said that once I decided to follow you, you would walk with me all the way, but I noticed that during the most troublesome times in my life there is only one set of footprints. I didn't understand why the times I needed you the most you would leave me." The Lord replied, "My precious, precious, child, I love you and would never ever leave you during your times of trial and despair. When you saw only one set of footprints, it was then that I carried you."

Don't spend a lot of time trying to understand; understanding is not the goal. Following God's lead is the goal. Do not listen to the sound. It is not the sound or the story, but the meaning. Do your best to figure out what is true and what is not. Winston Churchill spoke about how lies travel around the world while the truth is still putting on his shoes. He also said the farther backward you look, the farther forward you can see. Do not live in the past, but never forget it. Learn from it, and always try to do better.

I'm not only pro-life; I'm pro-eternal life. All life is important. We are all God's creatures; every living thing on this planet is important.

When I came home from Vietnam, I had a rifle and a shotgun. When Tom O'Brien turned twenty-five, I gave him my rifle and shotgun. Tom and Mike Longman enjoyed hunting and went duck, goose, and pheasant hunting every year. I'm glad they stay in touch and are still good friends.

When my good friend Jerry Miller, who lived next door to me in Eden Prairie, passed away, his wife Dee didn't want his guns in the house. I got a 300 Savage and a 911 .45 pistol. The main reason I wanted them was because they belonged to Jerry.

When we purchased a farm in Randolph, Minnesota, the previous owner had been dealing drugs out of the house. We did not know this at the time. For three years, people would show up at the farm looking for the stuff, as in, "You got the stuff, man?" By the time the police arrived, they were long gone. The police were very good about it and placed a police car at the end of our driveway. They used it for a radar trap to catch speeders. I think their physical presence help deter the drug dealers.

I met a Marine at Castle Rock bank when I was making a transaction one day. His name was Jerry Wicklund. We talked about where we served and when. He asked if I liked to hunt. I told him that I didn't anymore, but my son-in-law was always looking for a place to hunt. Jerry told me he owned 180 acres ten minutes to the west of us. We stayed in touch, and when hunting season came, he invited Matt to come hunting. Matt was so busy with work that he usually left the house at 6:30 a.m. and came home around 7:00 p.m. Matt said that we could use the deer meat. While he knew I was an excellent shot—I'm a qualified expert in the Marine Corps—he did not know I would have a hard time killing something. I decided if it would help put meat in the freezer, then I would give it a go. I got my hunting license and called Jerry Wicklund. He had cameras set up and saw deer every morning and at dusk. There was even a big buck that came by on a regular basis. I would go before sunrise and then back again before sunset. I spent many days sitting in the deer stand and never saw deer. I think the good Lord knew I was having second thoughts. I truly believe the good Lord kept all the deer away from that stand so I wouldn't have to kill anything.

CHAPTER 15

What to Do When You Retire

When Peg and I moved in together with Matt, Katie, William, and Isaac, the boys were very young. Peg and I interacted with them every day. As they grew up and started school, even though we were still in the same house, we very seldom interacted with the boys Monday through Friday. I needed a hobby to keep myself busy, so I started carving things out of wood. Then I made rubber binder guns. Eventually I evolved into making wooden toys. The first was a train with a steam engine, four cars, and a caboose. The second was another train with a diesel engine, four cars, and a caboose.

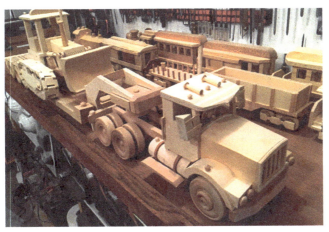

Wooden toys made by Bob Grant

Wooden tanker truck

The next two wooden toys were a bit harder. The first was a twenty-two-wheel tractor trailer. It took over a month to build. The next was a bulldozer that went on the flatbed trailer. This was all done inside of a little shop I built at the end of the pole barn. It is 15' x 22' long. I insulated and heated the shop, so I can work in the wintertime. The pole barn is 40' x 180'. It is split into three sections. Matt has sixteen feet, I have sixty feet, and the middle section we use for storage. The rest of my area outside of my heated shop I made into a man cave. While the house in Eden Prairie was pretty good size, we don't have a lot of room in the farmhouse. Many things had to go in the barn. I played sports for over thirty years and accumulated many trophies. The trophies are not worth anything, but the memories of the guys in the good times are priceless.

There are twelve sections in the man cave. Each section has a different theme.

Toy fire trucks

The first big section has over one hundred little firetrucks. Each one is all metal with many moving parts. Many come from the Franklin Mint and are collector pieces. I have many pictures to go along with the fire trucks and a few plaques: one for being Firefighter of the Year in Eden Prairie and one from the police department for helping set up safety camp and getting many things donated. The very first year of safety camp, I was a team leader, Katie was a helper, and Elizabeth was in the camp. Peg helped set up snacks and lunch and served the meal. I also received a plaque from the fire department for my many years of service.

Old pictures, fire trucks, old fire hats

I met the daughter of Henry E. Hansen; he had been fire chief in Minneapolis. Her dad had passed away, and she was cleaning out his house. She said he collected and kept everything. That sounded like me. I asked about what kind of stuff he kept, and she told me he was a fire chief and had many fire items like old helmets, badges, and pictures. She gave me many boxes full of his things. One was a leather helmet her dad wore when he first joined the department. You could tell it was really old and covered with soot. I can't imagine walking into a fire with a leather helmet! One of the old badges has a steamer and horses for its emblem. One Minneapolis fire badge has the date February 28, 1918. It also has the fireman's name on the badge: W.M. Flanery, Assistant Chief.

Fire badges

I have over one hundred badges in my collection and about a dozen helmets, including the leather one, a tin one, and plastic ones. I even kept the helmet I wore when I was an Eden Prairie fireman. All the badges are mounted on the wall in the man cave. I have a huge box of patches, both police and fire, that I have not mounted yet. Some of the old pictures of the Minneapolis Fire Department are pretty cool. One is a picture of the old steam engine being pulled by a team of four horses in full stride going down Hennepin Avenue. You can see the steam coming out of the steam engine, something you'll never see again. How cool is that? One picture is of the fire station that still has the wood floor inside. Many of these beautiful old stations are gone now.

The next section in the barn is a tribute to the Minnesota Twins. When I worked at the Eden Prairie Lund's store, I met a young man that was good friends with Gary Gaetti. My friend told Mr. Gaetti about me and that I was a Marine in Vietnam in 1968. He said Gary Gaetti wanted to meet me. The first time we met was at his friend's house in Eden Prairie. Mr. Gaetti was interested in my opinion about POWs. We got together on many different occasions. It was around that time that he reconnected with the good Lord. He had given up drinking and partying and was getting his life back on track. Peg and I really liked him, and I wish him well wherever he is today. I really felt he was a good role model for my two girls. He would give us four tickets to the Twins' home games. The seats were four rows up right behind home plate—the best seats in the house. When Gary would come out of the dugout, he would look over and tip his hat. I can't thank him enough. We were at game seven when the Twins won the World Series. That's why I have a section in my man cave dedicated to the Minnesota Twins and Gary Gaetti.

The next section in my man cave is a tribute to my mother-in-law, Millie Sherman. She left me the toy tractor collection that Steve, my father-in-law, had put together. I didn't ask for anything; this was her idea, and she wanted to give me something. I have collected about fifty old tractors. Some are from the 1950s and were made by the Charles William Doepke Manufacturing Company in Rossmoyne, Ohio. They are in excellent shape, and I have the brochure that goes with them. There is a road grader, a bottom dope excavator, and a farm implement that moves hay bales up into the loft.

Toy trucks

Toy tractors

The next section is a tribute to an old friend. I lived in Eden Prairie for thirty-four years. Next door to me lived Jerry and Dee Miller. Jerry worked for WCCO radio in downtown Minneapolis. He was the chief engineer for WCCO. Eventually he got bumped up to management. Just before he retired, he was inducted into the Radio Hall of Fame. While he worked for WCCO, he had an opportunity to meet many of the astronauts from the Gemini, Columbia, Challenger, and Apollo missions. He collected many patches, stamps, pictures, and signatures from the astronauts and had everything mounted by a professional framer. He had six big pictures on the wall in his family room and was really proud of that collection. He even had a forty-five record of the moon landing. One of the pictures in his collection was the prime crew for the first lunar landing. The three astronauts are Neil A. Armstrong, Michael Collins, and Edwin E. Aldrin Jr. When Jerry passed away from Lou Gehrig's disease, his wife Dee moved into a small house. She had no room to hang the collection, so she gave it to me. It all hangs in my man cave, and I think of Jerry every time I look at those things. You must see the collection to really appreciate it. Not only are there many patches of that era, but there are stamps that went with them.

The next section is a tribute to old cars and pictures of cars I once owned. On the wall is a picture of a 1965 Corvette. It was a red convertible with a red leather interior and red wall tires. The big framed picture in the middle is a picture of myself and my daughters Katie and Elizabeth in a 1957 Chevrolet pickup. The picture was taken in 1990 when the three of us went to "Back to the '50s" at the Minnesota State Fairgrounds. There were over ten thousand cars from the year 1963 and earlier; nothing was newer than 1963. There is also a picture of my youngest daughter Elizabeth in her 1963 Pontiac Bonneville. That was the first car she ever bought, and it was a beauty. When she drove it to college, the guys couldn't believe she had bought it, and it was hers. I have always enjoyed older cars. Today I drive a 1979 Ford F-100 pickup and a 1988 Cadillac de Ville that I bought for $4000. It's a beautiful car, and it only had thirty thousand original miles. The painting and interior are all original. You must see in person. The picture doesn't do it justice. There is no rust anywhere.

Old cars once owned

The next section is a tribute to twenty-five years of playing sports. It's made up of two shelves of trophies. They have no monetary value, but the memories and stories are priceless. There are pictures of Tom and Mike on the football team at Kennedy Park in South Minneapolis. The trophy for Coach of the Year is my favorite. It's one of the smallest on the shelf, but it means the most to me. I am missing a bunch of trophies that never made it to the farm. I don't know what happened to them.

The next section is a tribute to the veterans' memorial in Eden Prairie and includes a few pictures of the Vietnam War. The big frame picture in the middle is a picture of the flag raising at Iwo Jima. During the six years I was raising money for the veterans' memorial, I met Chuck Lindberg, who lived in Richfield and was one of the original Marines raising the flag at Iwo Jima. Inside the frame is a picture of Chuck signing the picture, so you know his signature is legitimate. He donated one of these to the Veterans Memorial Committee, and we auctioned it off. It helped raise a lot of money. I also bought two more prints from him, and I framed one. I still have the other, and I should frame it.

Chuck Lindberg was a Marine corporal who fought in three island campaigns during World War II. He was a member of the patrol that captured the top of Mount Suribachi where he helped raise the flag on the island on February 23, 1945. He was born on June 26, 1920, in Grand Forks, North Dakota. He died on June 24, 2007, in Edina, Minnesota and is buried at Fort Snelling National Cemetery. He was awarded the Purple Heart and the Silver Star.

There are also pictures of Vietnam in 1968. That was the year of the Tet Offensive. Some of the pictures include the destruction that occurred the night of the Tet, a picture of me flying gunner on a chopper, and a picture of me lying on the beach at a USO camp down in southern Vietnam. We received five days R&R (rest and relaxation) outside of Vietnam; I went to Singapore and Malaysia. We also received one day in-country R&R and one phone call that lasted three minutes. That was the only mental escape in 395 days. I put these pictures up on the wall, hoping that my grandchildren would someday understand.

Margaret E. Grant

The next section is a tribute to my beautiful bride. I had a professional photographer take pictures of her when she was in her twenties. Even though she's a bit younger in the pictures, she's just as beautiful today. She is the glue that helped hold me together. I never would've made it without her. When I prayed to God in 1968, I never thought my dream would come true. She has done a wonderful job raising our two girls. She has a way about her, calm and in control. She did day care for many years. These young kids would come to our home as newborns and stay until they went off to school. Many of them came back to see her and had nothing but nice things to say about her when we went to their high school and college graduations. I don't think we had just two kids; I think we had about thirty. We get Christmas cards every year from the parents of those kids.

Day Care, Peg's kids

Even though my two girls have homes of their own, we are still a big part of their lives. If they ever need my help, they both know that Peg and I will be there always. I know that Elizabeth will someday get married and have children. Elizabeth is a beautiful young lady who is involved with church and has a good job and a beautiful, three-bedroom, three-bath home in Eden Prairie. I'm not sure if I will see that day. That's one of the reasons I started writing this, so someday my grandkids can pick up this memoir and read about their grandpa.

Katie, my oldest daughter, is amazing. She is married with three children, runs a household, helps her husband with their business, homeschools their two boys, and has the patience to be a great mom for little Evy. When Katie was in college, she majored in international business and Japanese heritage, culture, and language. During her senior year, she studied overseas in Osaka, Japan. Her host family did not speak English, so she had to speak Japanese and became fluent.

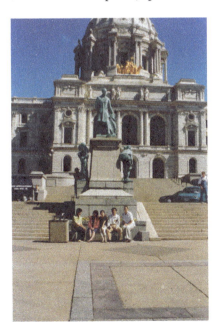

The Olympics were held in Japan that year. There were many tickets available for the Olympics, but the bullet train to get to the Olympics was sold out. The host family got tickets for the bullet train for Katie and her friends. When the China-USA women's hockey game was on television, Peg and I were sitting at the dining room table doing paperwork. Peg looked up and said, "Oh my god, it's Katie on national television!" Because the USA women's team was rated number one and the women's China hockey team had not won a game, Katie and her friends were the only Americans at the game. The network filming the game went to Katie and her friends and told them every time the USA scored a goal, they would be putting the cameras on them. They were supposed to stand up, wave the American flag, and cheer for the Americans. The USA women's hockey team scored five times, and each time, Katie and her friends were on national television. It was so exciting for us to see her on television that we wrote to the network and had them send us a copy of the game on a DVD.

When Katie finished her year in Japan, I sent the host family a nice gift for taking such good care of our daughter. The host family wrote me a letter and thanked me for the gift. They were planning a trip to America and asked if they could stay with us. Sure! The family flew into San Francisco where they stayed for a day. Then they flew into Las Vegas where they stayed for a day. Then they flew into Minneapolis. We picked them up at the airport, and they stayed with us for five days. We showed them downtown Minneapolis, toured the Minnesota State Capitol and the Basilica in St. Paul, and drove around Lake Harriet, Lake Calhoun, and Lake of the Isles. They couldn't believe all the big homes around Lake of the Isles.

One of my friends on the fire department was Brian McGraw. His dad, Neil, owned a forty-two-feet cruiser on Lake Minnetonka. Neil McGraw offered to take us all on a cruise around Lake Minnetonka. Peg fixed a turkey for lunch on the boat. When we cruised by Pillsbury Point where there is only one home and a huge yard, the Japanese family commented on the nice hotel. Katie replied that it was a home. They asked how many families lived there, and

Katie explained that there was only one. They couldn't believe it! When they first arrived in Minnesota, we took them to our house and went into the backyard. They thought it was a nice park. We explained it was our backyard. The homes in Japan have no yards at all, and the houses are so close together that, according to Katie, you have to walk sideways to walk between them. Our Japanese friends said they loved Minnesota the best because of all the lakes and beautiful yards.

We went to a restaurant one morning, and I ordered almost everything on the menu to give them a taste of an American breakfast. The waitress told us we ordered way too much. What she didn't know was that our guests ate far more than we do. When we finished breakfast, there wasn't a smidgen left. The family told us that if we ever go to Japan, we can stay with them. In Japan, only the top 10 percent of all students applying to college are accepted. This was probably the biggest vacation they had ever planned, but their oldest son stayed behind in Japan, so he could study for the test to go to college.

My wife Peg is going to live to be at least one hundred. I don't think I will be able to see and meet all of our grandkids. I don't think the good Lord has that in my playbook. I have always said that if today's the day, I won't whine and cry or ask for a few more hours or a few more days. I will thank him for time served.

I also have a section of the barn dedicated to our family tree. I have 506 names dating back to 1680. I put pictures on the wall of our grandparents, great-grandparents, and great-great-grandparents. When William and Isaac hear about family, they can actually go to my man cave and see a picture of them. There are many pictures of the Hansen, Grant, and Sherman clans. When we bought property in Randolph, it left a lot to be desired. The house was condemned, most of the windows were broken, the copper was ripped out, and only one toilet worked. When my grandchildren get older, they can look back at forty to fifty pictures on the wall in my man cave to see what the farm looked like when we bought it.

As we come to the end of my story, you've probably figured out this wasn't written by some professor or college student who graduated top in his class. I'm just an everyday guy. My youngest daughter

Elizabeth knows me best. She gave me a sign that I put up over the door to my shop, which says, *Just plowing along.* When my doctor told me to get my life in order, I felt the need to finish my book and take a hard look back at my life. I started thinking about those footprints in the sand. Have I left any footprints that may be remembered or may have made a difference in someone's life? If you want to give credit where credit is due, all the credit must go to God who first saved me that night of the Tet Offensive and then guided me down this path called my life.

I know the day is coming when I will see my father who I lost at a young age, my mom, my brother, and all the family and friends I lost over the years. If today's the day, I could not and would not ask for anything more. I am truly thankful for what the good Lord has given me, and I am glad that he allowed me to walk this path.

There are stories and sayings I read or heard over the years that help guide me down that path of life. Here are a few:

- Wooden ships, sailing ships, ships that sailed the seas, the most important is friendship, may it always be. (George W. Bush)
- Faith means more than words. It means service to family, friends, and God.
- Chinese zodiac is a twelve-year cycle. The year of the dog is 1946. I was born in 1946! Loyal and honest, works well with others, generous but stubborn, and often selfish; look out for the dragon, and look for the horse or tiger. Margaret Elizabeth Sherman, my wife, was born 1950, the year of the tiger. Tiger people are aggressive, courageous, candid, and sensitive. It was a good match.
- Those who were hurt the worst have the greatest ability to heal.
- We don't get to choose what happens to us. We do get to choose how it shapes us.
- Everything comes and goes. Nothing comes to stay.
- What doesn't kill you will make you stronger.

- Some people spend their entire lifetime wondering if they have made a difference. Marines don't have that problem. (President Ronald Reagan)
- The hardest things in life have the best rewards. (Kalab at the Children's Hospital)
- The best way to help yourself is to put your arm around someone who needs it more.
- What lies behind us and what lies before us is a tiny matter compared to what lies within us. (Ralph Waldo Emerson)
- The rearview mirror on your windshield is very small. Why? Because what's behind you isn't as important as what's out in front of you.

I did not spend a lot of time trying to understand because understanding is not the goal. Following God's lead is the goal.

I did not and do not preach Christ. I preach by example. I am far from being perfect, and I never told anyone I was. In all my years, I have met many people who thought they were, but I have never known one that was. I hope you will not judge me by my mistakes. I have tried my best with what I've had. We don't get to choose what happens to us; we do get to choose how it shapes us.

When you are closer to the end than the beginning, you ask yourself some questions: Have I made a difference? What kind of footprints have I left behind?

I want to thank the good Lord for leading me down the many paths of life. I have made many friends and have many fond memories. You will be in my thoughts each and every day until Judgment Day.

CHAPTER 16

Hope

I am not writing this book to make me rich, yet I hope it does generate a lot of revenue. I have a few bills I want to pay, and then the majority of the money from each book sold will go to my two daughters and to help make Evelyn Elizabeth Hansen's life a little better. The home that Katie and Matt moved into was condemned at the time and had broken windows, broken doors, a failed furnace, and a frozen well. Not only will I set money aside for little Evelyn, but also, I will do my best to improve the conditions around the property.

If you read my book and you think it's worth reading, please recommend it to all your family and friends. Please do everything you can to make this a best seller. Please tell everyone at work and church to buy a copy of this book. I want money set aside in case something happens to Matt or Katie, so little Evelyn will always be taken care of.

Thank you, and I hope you enjoyed the book.

Bob Grant, Viet Nam

Bob and Peg Grant, back to the 50's; 1990

Elizabeth Wells Grant; first car, bought with her own money

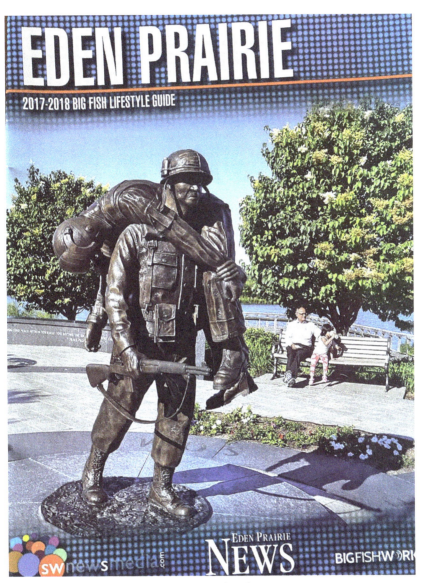

Veteran's Memorial, Eden Prairie

Cover of Police Chief's magazine.
Bob Grant; yellow cap; back row, center.

ABOUT THE AUTHOR

A lost soul, never to be seen again!

When Robert was a young boy living in South Minneapolis, he thought everyone had three square meals a day and went to bed with clean sheets every night. He never thought about the effects of a draft notice or being shipped off to war could have on him. When he came home from Vietnam, the house was gone and all the furniture in it. Everything they ever owned was gone. His mom never worked a day in her life; she was now $37,000 in debt. He made a promise to his father; he would take care of his mom. He came home from Vietnam with so much baggage; he had no idea how to make this work. He took one day at a time, one foot in front of the other, with no long-term plan.

The first night of the Tet Offensive, Vietnam 1968, when he gave his life, his physical being, and his soul to the good Lord, little did he know he would be there with him every step of the way.

Has his life made a difference? Will anyone even notice?

1. The loss of his father as a boy
2. United States Marine Corps: Vietnam 1967–1968
3. Buying a house and taking care of his mom
4. Coaching football
5. Big Brothers Big Sisters of America
6. Eden Prairie Fire Department
7. Firefighter of the Year 1995
8. CERT Team member, Eden Prairie, Minnesota
9. Governor's Emergency Response Commission
10. Schreiner

11. Vice chair, Veterans Memorial Committee
12. Raised $618,000.00 for the veterans memorial
13. Operation Honor Guard—VFW, American Legion

CPSIA information can be obtained
at www.ICGtesting.com
Printed in the USA
LVHW072004200322
713947LV00001B/1